PUBLI~~~~

Remarkable
Occurrences

BORN 4 APRIL 1848 YAZOO COUNTY, MISSISSIPPI
DIED 1931 WESTMONT, ILLINOIS
HE WAS SAVED JULY 12, 1874 (SEE P. 16, "SANCTIFICATION,")
HE WAS SANCTIFIED JUNE 1, 1889 (SEE PP. 4, 13, "SANCTIFICATION,")
9 AM, AGE 41, NEW ORLEANS, UNDER THE EARLIER PREACHING
OF W. W. HOPPER.

By

Beverly Carradine (A MAN)

*Author of "Golden Sheaves," "Gideon," "Jonah," "Pen Pictures,"
"Pastoral Sketches," "A Journey to Palestine," "Soul Help," "Heart
Talks," "Sanctification," "The Second Blessing in Symbol," "The Better
Way," "The Old Man," "The Bottle," "Church Entertainments," "The
Lottery," "The Sanctified Life" and "Revival Sermons."*

ISBN 0-88019-323-9

Schmul Publishing Co., Inc.
Wesleyan Book Club   1994   Salem, Ohio

Printed by
Old Paths Tract Society
Route 2, Box 43
Shoals, IN 47581

Contents

Remarkable Occurrences

I.

The Strange Case of Doctor Broad

The title "Doctor" as used above was not a medical but a theological designation. The subject of this sketch was a preacher. He had been D. D.'d and LL. D'd and was about forty years of age when we first saw him. He always wore the regulation clergyman's coat with its single row of buttons and long skirt, carried an ebony cane in his right hand, or hooked with its curved handle to his arm, while the left hand clothed with one glove held its mate folded up nicely in the same palm.

Black-haired, black-eyed, with glossy Burnside whiskers, and fine erect figure, he was a man who impressed everyone by his very presence. When in addition we mention that he had a superior intellect, and whatever he said on platform or in pulpit was thoughtful and well worth remembering, it can easily be seen how and why he took a prominent position speedily and naturally in the assemblies and conventions of his church. The chairmanship of committees seemed to be given to him as a matter of course, and when he arose to speak in the annual gathering of the preachers on matters of church business, it was noticed that not only the delegates listened but the president or chairman of the entire body always fixed his eyes upon the speaker and heard him silently and thoughtfully to the last word.

Besides the man's intellectual and linguistic gifts, he possessed a most gracious and ingratiating manner. He was cordial to everyone alike, seemed to know everybody, and from the frequent handshakes that he gave and received, it was seen why the right glove had to be carried in the left hand. Meantime, while open and kindly to all, there were different shades of treatment given to those of different ages and classes and characters, which showed the discriminating eye and mind of the man. To the old he showed that respect and attention which is so grateful to people in that time of life; and to the young an affability and interest which was not less pleasing and delightful to them. His bearing to rich and poor, to the scholarly and ignorant, was just what it should have been, and was in the judgment of many beyond criticism.

As we are writing of a very strange case, one of life's mysteries in fact, it is well for the reader to note carefully each expression we use.

As a preacher he was always edifying; as a pastor diligent and attentive. His congregation was devoted, we came very near saying worshiped him. His leading members were simply wrapped up in the man. He baptized all their babies and married all their sons and daughters. He was continually "dined" by his friends, graced all their state occasions, and never seemed blander and more delightful than at such times.

At these great dinings, where the company sat at the board from two to three hours, where there were seven or more courses and wine throughout, Doctor Broad drank one or two small glasses without any scruple and never dreamed of denying the fact. Afterwards he would retire to the library with the gentlemen and, while smoking a cigar with them, would enter into discussions concerning the leading questions, problems and events of the day.

The Doctor also smoked at home in his Study, and likewise at his Conference. He was a man who never concealed anything he did. He did not indulge the weed to what is called excess, but smoked as a rule three times a day. On social occasions he increased the number to the fourth or fifth cigar. It was also noticeable that he used the best Havanas.

He was repeatedly seen in attendance upon the County and State fairs. He seemed deeply interested in the products of the farm and factory, and all the works of human skill and ingenuity. Once he was seen watching a horse race near the grand stand.

Doctor Broad was a great lodge or fraternity man. He had gone as far in Masonry as possible and stood very high in the estimation of that body of men. He seemed to take a genuine pleasure in these associations, and when he was in his regalia, and figured prominently in one of the uniformed and brass-banded processions, while he always conducted himself with great dignity, yet it was evident that he was delighted with the whole thing. He seemed to be in his element. The portrait of himself which he most prized, and which was hung up over the mantel in the parlor of the parsonage, represented him all covered and glittering with the showy dress of some high office in the Masonic fraternity.

He never opposed any of the fairs and festivals which his leading lady members saw fit to have in his church. He attended them all, and beamed pleasantly and graciously on everybody present.

It was commented on freely that Doctor Broad never had what is called a real revival in his different charges; and yet he always brought up every collection in full, and had such additions each year that the church kept up its financial and numerical strength. Moreover, the leading society people of the town always came to hear him, while prominent professional men, lawyers and doctors, and the gifted and brainy tribe of the community thickly sprinkled his congregation. For another preacher to arise in Doctor Broad's place on some Sabbaths was the signal for a number in the audience to withdraw.

And so the Doctor went on his way until he was a gray-haired man of sixty. The Burnsides were white but the expressive black eyes glowed the same and the fiery end of the cigar continued to gleam from the mouth.

If possible, Doctor Broad was blander than ever, more popular with the people, and had greater influence in the Bishop's
cabinet and on the floor of the Conference.

He was received without a question by his different flocks
as a whole, who were always glad to have him returned; but he
was also a puzzle and a problem to certain individuals, and did
not take with the deeply spiritual of the membership.

This last fact never seemed to affect him, however, and
never caused him to cut them or be unkind in any way. Indeed,
he was peculiarly courteous and gracious to these non-admirers.

One Sabbath a young preacher filled the pulpit of Doctor
Broad at the latter's urgent entreaty. The Doctor's health had
been failing for some months, so that the request was not surprising or unprecedented. He sat in the pulpit, however, while
the young preacher, with his heart on fire with the Holy Spirit,
preached from the text, "It is appointed unto men once to die,
and after that the Judgment." It was the Communion Sabbath
and the table, with its white cloth covering the bread and wine,
was before him in the altar. Doubtless the subject of "Death and
the Judgment" was not appropriate, but nevertheless the Holy
Ghost came upon the Word in a solemn and even awful way. The
whole audience became as still as death, and conviction as deep
as it was unusual fell upon the people. The congregation, unused
to such preaching, looked not only uncomfortable but disturbed
and offended, not to say outraged.

At the conclusion of the sermon the preacher sat down with
the conviction that while God was with him, other forces which
he could not understand were against him. Doctor Broad arose
and, leaning against the Bible stand, proceeded to give a soothing talk of ten or fifteen minutes. A sigh of relief seemed to go
up from the congregation the instant he opened his mouth. He
said "That it was true, as the preacher had said in his sermon,
which he had greatly enjoyed, that Death had to come, and after
that the Judgment with Christ upon the throne; but before those
two solemn occasions, the blessed opportunity of salvation was

granted us; and that, while Christ was to be the Judge, yet thus far He was the Friend of Sinners, the Saviour, Advocate, Intercessor and Comforter of us all." He then drew a picture of Jesus upon the cross, talked of His love to us, and our loyalty to Him, and then invited the people to the altar to take the Supper of the Lord.

The transformation of feeling was speedy and complete in the mental and spiritual realm of the audience, and the change was wrought by the speaker not only without reflection upon the young preacher, but even with complimentary references to him. Still the effect of the pulpit message was wiped out, and the messenger could not but feel that he had been politely but certainly stabbed. The congregation, now restored to ease of mind and its usual good-humor and self-complacency, did not give him another thought; and he, after the service, walked away unnoticed by the throng which surged about the chancel to shake hands with Doctor Broad.

A few months after this the Doctor was stretched upon his dying bed. Always kind and courteous in life, he was considerate and thoughtful of others in the sick room. He said nothing about his spiritual condition, but said "Amen" very heartily to the prayers offered at his bedside by different ministers for his recovery, and for the blessing of God upon him and his family.

On the twentieth day of his sickness he died. He had full possession of his faculties to the last, and spoke quietly and cheerfully to those sitting or standing near him up to a few minutes before he passed away, when suddenly, a kind of mental shock seemed to take place, and his great black eyes became fixed on something before and somewhat above him, as though in wonder and even horror. Mixed with the astonishment and fear was an expression seen upon faces when an unexpected turn of events or an undreamed of catastrophe has broken upon them. No one versed in spiritual things could look upon the convulsed face and startled, dilated eyes of Doctor Broad without seeing that a strange new light had broken in upon the man; that discoveries were taking place or disclosures being made; that in a word he was going through some tremendous and fearful experience, and yet had passed the line where the tongue is allowed to declare the mysteries of the other world. And so, without another word, but with that amazed, shocked look in his eyes, to which the dropping chin added in startled appearance, the soul of Doctor Broad left his body and went, as shall be the case with us all, to the place prepared by the life and character.

The church had very little to do with the funeral of the Doctor; for the various fraternities to which he belonged pushed in and took entire charge of the final melancholy arrangements. There were two brass bands in the long procession, while white aprons, flashing regalias, beribboned wands, and waving banners abounded. Fulsome speeches and addresses were made over the flower-covered coffin in the large city hall; the bands wailed their dirges along the streets; and after considerable ceremony at the grave, the earth was thrown in, the head-board set up, the floral wreaths and crosses laid on the mound, and the great crowd dispersed and left Doctor Broad six feet under the sod to await the sound of the trumpet ushering in the morning of the Resurrection and the Great Day of the Final Judgment.

A group of five men lingered a few moments at the gate of the cemetery before taking their departure for home, store and farm.

One said, "If they realize in the other world what is going on in this, then Doctor Broad is a happy man; for if he knows that his funeral procession was a half mile long, had two brass bands and four fraternities in line, then he is glad, I don't care where he is."

The second man said, "I never heard Doctor Broad say an unkind thing about anybody in all the many years I have known him."

The third individual added, "While Doctor Broad smoked cigars and drank an occasional glass of wine, I would far rather have his kind spirit and risk his chance in the other world, than to be like some people who criticized and abused him all his life. I think it is less harm to smoke a cigar, than to burn up the reputation and usefulness and happiness of a man or a woman by a caustic, bitter tongue, which is itself set on fire of hell."

The fourth person remarked solemnly, "I believe that in the moment of death Doctor Broad saw he had made a horrible and irreparable mistake; that he had missed the real Christ life; in a word, that he had lost his soul."

The fifth man said, "If the false prophets and shepherds whom the Bible speaks of are lost, then Doctor Broad is lost. If the people who cry for mercy at the Judgment Day, saying 'Lord, Lord, did we not preach in Thy name in the streets, and in Thy name do many wonderful works,' and yet will hear Christ declaring, 'I know you not,' and shall straightway fall into an endless Perdition; even so I believe that Doctor Broad on that day will stagger backward from the face and words of the Son of God and fall headlong into a bottomless hell."

The men parted; the gate was closed; the sound of the last wheel died away in the distance; and the cemetery with its fragrant breath of Cape Jasmine and Magnolia blossoms, with its sighing willows, and vacant seats and walks, was left silent and solitary once more, with the latest addition to its white-faced sleepers in the pulseless, rigid form of Doctor Broad.

II.

A Prince in Israel

Souls are said to be equally precious on account of being made in the likeness of God, redeemed by the same Blood, and with immortal natures susceptible of endless development and improvement.

Yet just as true is it that some souls are worth more to humanity and God than others. Two brothers are converted and both gain heaven, but one simply saved himself and the other brought a great company with him. Two members of a church, and in the same social plane, receive full salvation, but one exerts only a small influence in his community, while the other affects his entire neighborhood or town, and hundreds will rise up and call him blessed at the last day. Sometimes one person's conversion or sanctification means more to this world than a revival which swept a thousand into salvation. The one accomplished more in after life than did the entire ten hundred.

In addition to immortal and Christ-redeemed natures, there are such things as boundless energy, a vigorous intellect, a refined nature, good breeding, gentlemanly instincts, a high sense of honor, character, studious habits, and a life of prayer. Such men or women move easily and naturally to the front, and they stand out from amid their fellows as did the patriarchs in their day, the prophets in their time, the disciples in the first century, and that devoted band of men who gave to the world the Wesleyan Revival.

The longer we live the more convinced we are as we see narrowness contrasted with broadness, laziness over against energy, helpfulness assisted by helpfulness, that there is a great difference among souls.

With the profoundest belief in inbred sin and total depravity, with all the contradictory and confusing facts and figures along the line of the ancestry argument, yet it remains that some men are born gentlemen, and as far back as we can trace them in childhood possess noble, trustful, manly characters.

Among this latter class was a country boy, in one of our Southern States, whose baptismal name was Edward. He started life with a sound body, a splendid mind, a noble heart, excellent business gifts or qualifications, and a spirit full of industry and perseverance. Crowning and beautifying all was a blessed Christian experience, which he retained through a life of over eighty years, and which we have never doubted, in view of his deeds, was one of full salvation.

The first time his wife ever saw him he was driving a team of oxen yoked to a large wagon. She was taking a horseback ride with a party of young friends and dashed past the loaded vehicle, little dreaming that the youth walking by the side of the steers and popping his whip as he stood on the big wagon tongue, was her future husband. She galloped on out of sight with her merry companions, but Edward, even then with his mind full of noble, grand thoughts, came quietly and steadily after, driving up the road in a deeper sense than the literal one, and not only approaching the mission of his life, but entering upon its blessed accomplishment so as to win the favor of men and the blessings of heaven.

It is wonderful what he overtook on that road. He soon passed in trueness of living the young men, who loped by him that morning. He left many others beside them behind. He overtook the girl who became his wife. He overtook fortune. He caught up with public honor and general respect. He swept on to still greater wealth, and possessed broad plantations and a beautiful mansion home. At the same time he walked unbrokenly with God. His earthly abundance failed to come in between him and his Saviour. The remarkable thing soon noticed by everybody was that the more he prospered financially the more he gave to God.

He did not do like a man we know who, as he made money, would invest it in partial purchases, so as to say to seekers after his bounty that he was in debt. He did not let the money which flowed in metallize his soul, as it has done to many; but as God prospered him he gave. The more his business increased, the greater swelled his streams of gold and silver in gifts to God, and benevolence to men.

It looked like God had found a man He could trust with riches, and so He smiled upon and blessed every enterprise of His faithful servant. The Almighty fairly rained wealth on him, and he showered it back. It looked to heaven and to spiritual observers that a kind of love and trust struggle was going on between the two. God would seem to be saying:

"Here, my son, is more money for you. I know you will not worship it; nor let it make you cold and haughty to your fellow-beings; nor cause you to cease leaning on Me. Here is a large amount for you." And the true follower of Christ, who had not lost his head with his great successes, not surrendered his love for the Saviour or his fellow-creatures, would let the dollars fly in thousands to help the bodies of men on earth, and their souls on the way to heaven.

He put sixty thousand dollars in one church. He gave one hundred thousand to a college. There was scarcely a house of worship within a hundred miles of his home but had his means in it from fifty to one thousand dollars. The preachers knew where to come when financial help was needed for the sick and the poor. His purse was ever open to the cry of want.

Not a minister of the Gospel in that Southern State, or from any other State, but was assured of and always received a cordial welcome in the elegant, hospitable house of the subject of this sketch. Sometimes these clerical and lay guests were poorly clad, and unpolished and awkward in manner, but their noble-hearted entertainer never seemed to notice it, and treated the poorest man who accepted his hospitality with the same courtesy and cordial-ity that he did one of the neighboring wealthy cotton planters.

On one occasion an humble guest, in tilting back his chair on the waxed floor of the parlor, came near losing his balance and falling on the floor. Two of the daughters of the household gave a little snicker peculiar to the senselessness of youth, but the grave, rebuking look of their father settled them instantly then and there. Then, as if nothing had happened, the courtly, noble man, who had been a poor boy in the beginning of his life, said to his confused guest:

"These waxed floors are a pet idea of my wife and daughters. I have pleaded in vain for carpets all the year round for safety's sake; for even now, after the practice of years, I walk over these slippery floors almost in terror of my life. But they are the queens of the home, and I submit to their superior taste at the risk of a fractured limb or a broken head."

The relief of the guest was immediate, while the speech was so kind and pleasant as to inflict no wound on the family, in coming to the deliverance of the friend or acquaintance.

A number of preachers who at different times spent the night at this home famous for its hospitality, would leave next day with an experience which was made up of equal parts of surprise and pleasure, and caused a general laugh over the neighborhood when it was found out. If any of them came on a poor, broken-down horse and left him tied at the rack, this was the last he ever saw of the animal, for next morning, in taking his departure, there, at the hitching place where he had left a bundle of skin and bones with an old saddle upon it, was a handsome, well-kept steed, and freshly caparisoned.

"Why, where is my horse?" he would say in astonishment. "Some mistake has been made." But the servant told him that there had been no mistake; that "Ole Marster" had made him this present.

Then the next words would be, "I want to see your 'marster' "—"this is too kind"—or, "I want to thank him," etc., etc. But by this time Judge M., for this was the title given him after middle life, was not to be seen; he had vanished. As for the old animal which had disappeared, the Judge superannuated him, and set him free, letting him eat, graze and roll out the balance of his days without work, in view of what he had done.

When the Civil War broke out in 1861, Judge M. greatly helped the Confederate cause. His factory supplied blankets, and his broad acres yielded food for the soldiers. It was said by one who knew him well that he took care of the family of every poor Southern soldier in a radius of twelve miles of his home.

Such was his powerful help in various ways to the cause of the South that, when a Federal raid swept through that part of the State where he lived in the latter part of the war, he was arrested and taken out in front of his house to be shot.

A file of soldiers was selected to do the shooting, and Judge M., now silver-haired and eighty, was placed before them, sitting in a chair because of his feebleness, to receive their bullets.

The grand old man, with his gray hair falling upon his shoulders, looked like a patriarch, as he sat quietly facing the Union soldiers. He was as calm as when he had entertained his guests upon the gallery or in the parlor, and dispensed the hospitality for which he was famous. Even now he looked more like a prince receiving visitors than a condemned man facing a death-guard and executioners.

Three times the eight men raised their guns at the command of their officer to "Make ready," "Aim," and "Fire!" And three times their Enfield rifles dropped! They could not pull the trigger; they could not fire!

Would the reader like to know why?

It was not only because of the kind and noble face shining upon them; but there was something between them and the victim. Something that they could not move away, nor shoot through. This something was the Word of God!

The special passage was Psalm 41, verses 1 and 2, "Blessed is the man that considereth the poor; the Lord will deliver him in time of trouble. The Lord will preserve him and keep him alive; and he shall be blessed upon the earth; and thou wilt not deliver him unto the will of his enemies."

The man before them had cared for the poor all his life; he had won God's promise of protection and deliverance; and now, according to God's own Word, they could not do him any harm. He was as safe from their bullets as though he was in heaven.

Judge M. lived a few years after this and passed away into the skies in great peace and triumph. Like Jacob he was old and full of days; like Enoch he walked with God and was not, for God took him; and like Abel he being dead yet speaketh.

III.

The Warmed Serpent

In one of our Southern States there lived a prosperous farmer. He had a pleasant cottage home, with orchard, garden, yards, and barns, while stretching beyond these possessions were twenty-five acres of cotton and corn.

He was a married man with one little girl. He had professed religion at some protracted or camp meeting, and joined the Methodist Church. The life he lived was a quiet and simple one, but he had the necessaries of life, with comforts besides, had his church associations and privileges, with pleasant neighbors, was fairly prosperous and a contented man.

One night he heard a knock at his front door. On going to the steps he found a tramp standing in the dark, who asked for his supper and a night's lodging. Mr. K. told him to come in. The man did so, and instead of spending one night, he stayed thirty-three years. He passed the rest of his life in that home, and only left it as a corpse a generation of years later. He not only did this, but, fearful to relate, stole away the Christian faith of his entertainer; morally and spiritually ruined him, and landed his soul in perdition.

The man was a tramp, but no ordinary one. He was bright, brainy and well-read, but without the inclination to make his own living; a character that is not infrequently met with in society, where the shiftless individual is smart and entertaining, but reluctant to work with hands or brain for daily bread. Such men become hangers on of families, spongers upon friends, making themselves agreeable and even desirable by their quick wits, and only requiring in pay that they get their bed and board. Many of these persons are not harmful, but are simply barnacles clinging to those who will allow them to be such social attachments.

In the case mentioned in this sketch, the man who knocked at the door and stayed thirty-three years was a bad man. He was a skeptic dyed in the wool, and had the writings of Paine and Voltaire at his fingers' ends.

It took some time, but he accomplished his infernal work at last, and utterly destroyed the Christian faith and experience of the man who bade him come in out of the night. He was the serpent warmed at the hearth that returned the kindness of his benefactor by stinging him to spiritual death. He made a horrible return for the kindness shown him in his need.

Mr. K. gave up the church, worked about his farm on the Sabbath, became a tobacco worm, and developed into a gloomy-faced, sour-spirited, bitter-tongued man. Many of his acquaintances and friends fell away from him, and he was thrown mainly, and finally almost entirely, upon the infidel for company.

At last the skeptic died, and the gray-haired man in the coffin in the wagon was followed by a gray-haired man on horseback as the solitary mourner.

After this Mr. K. became still more morose and bitter, hardly ever leaving his farm and so almost literally dropped out of public sight and notice.

Four years after the death of the tramp who had ruined him, he himself was taken down with a desperate sickness. He lingered in great suffering for several weeks. The writer arriving at that time as the pastor of a church in a neighboring town, was sent for to visit him. The summons came on the day of the old man's death. Not having a horse, and unable to borrow one, and realizing the urgency of the case, we trudged on foot four miles along a muddy road to the house of death.

The sick, or, rather, dying man, was conscious, but refused to talk. We knelt and prayed for him, and the prayer seemed driven back in our face. Arising from our knees, we begged him to accept Christ, and he with a black and horrible look rejected Him. In a few minutes more he was a corpse. Two days later he was buried in a country graveyard, and near the church which he had attended in his happier days.

It was the custom of the neighborhood to remove the coffin lid at the graveyard and let the people pass in a kind of procession by the casket and take a farewell look at the deceased. On that day there happened to be two burials, and both occurring at the same hour. One was that of Mr. K., and the other the funeral of a saintly lady aged about eighty.

Separated by about twenty yards, the two coffins were placed on the ground and the lids removed. Several hundred people looked at the two silent forms and will never forget as long as eternity rolls the striking and even fearful difference between the two death-touched countenances. The glory actually lingered on the face of that Mother in Israel who had walked with God without a break for over sixty years.

Scarcely a soul that day looked upon the calm, sweet and all but smiling face without tears springing to the eyes. God's seal was on His own, even in death.

The crowd, after the burial of this Daughter of the King, went over to Mr. K's grave lot, where the casket lay upon the grass with its silent tenant inside. The cover was removed, and the people marched by its side and, glancing in, instantly averted their eyes with looks of pain and distress, and some even with low exclamations of horror. The face had on it the very same black scowl that we saw a few minutes before death. It was an expression so dark and hopeless and hard that we do not believe a single one doubted that the man was lost. The soul in quitting the body seemed to have left its own terror and despair upon the face as it fled away into eternal night.

The question asked by some would be, why did God allow such a being to come to that house and forever ruin the man who was kind to him?

The Bible plainly answers all such questions, while life is full of similar instances, and the word Probation contains in itself a perfect explanation to any thoughtful and sensible man.

Judge Longstreet, a prominent educator in the South, tells of a gifted young man who married a fashionable girl at a time when his prospects were brilliant and success assured. The woman was a mere butterfly of fashion, had no idea how to keep a house, preside at the table, or save money. The husband brought his friends home to dine with him, as he was a public character, and his mortifications were so deep and frequent on these occasions, and his bills became so great, run up by the thoughtless, giddy, foolish woman he had married, that he finally took to drink, and in a few years, after having lost all his practice and property, landed in a drunkard's grave.

Again the question comes up, why did not God prevent all this by removing the weak, vain, useless girl before she met the young and gifted lawyer? And again we are answered by the word, Probation.

We look at the silly marriages of godly women to worldly, sinful men, and the senseless matches made by preachers with women who are neither companions nor helpmeets to their husbands, and we wonder what they were thinking of at the time. Such ill-assorted relations mean not only unhappiness to both, but oftentimes backsliding and moral shipwreck. We have known good men to go to ruin through an unhappy marriage. An unspiritual woman stood on the doorstep, knocked, was admitted, took possession, and drove a man of God to desperation, sin and the grave of a backslider. She herself followed the body of the man she had ruined to the tomb. Maybe she sat in the carriage behind a black crepe veil and wiped her eyes with a black-bordered handkerchief. But she was the murderess of the man in the coffin, just the same.

And God allows all this, because it is a part of our probation. We are on trial. We are being tested in many ways. If we cannot stand temptation, we ought to know it. If we cannot rise superior to wrong influences, how can we be rewarded, much less saved? If people have to be killed, or we must be caught up into the skies from the presence of every man or woman who comes along, how can we be tried and tested, how find out what is in us, and how develop the spiritual powers that lie all dormant and unknown within us?

So the mistakes in marriage, business, and other momentous matters are permitted. The man or woman who is to injure or ruin us is allowed to knock at the door of the life. And this is partly to test us, but also because there is no need for us to stagger and fall. He that is for us is greater than the person who stands at the door and comes into the life. If we look to Christ, no one can pluck us from His hand.

IV.

The Two Letters

In our early ministerial life we had a member of our church who was a steward and trustee, the friend of the preacher, prayed well, paid well, was a good leader of a prayer meeting, and stood high as a citizen and Christian in the small town where he lived.

He had a very wild, wicked son, and two superior and attractive daughters. These two last undoubtedly made a bright home for the father. Both were handsome, intelligent girls, but he seemed to be especially fond of the elder of the two. This preference was evident to everybody, and the daughter herself felt that she was the favorite.

Meantime the son gave nothing but trouble in his short visits home, or in his long absences, no one knew where. One thing was clearly demonstrated in this case, and that was that locality and surroundings failed to affect him for good; he was a transgressor of human and divine law wherever he went.

The daughters seemed in a measure to take the son's place and greatly brightened the home, so that it was a pleasure to visit the house and listen to the cheerful conversation of the father, who was quite a reader and thinker, and unquestionably a superior man. It was touching to see his love and fondness for his daughters, and especially noticeable how his eyes shone in approval and admiration of the elder girl. He had gotten in some way to lean upon her, and she had willingly become a stay to this man of sixty.

One morning the village was shocked at the tidings that his favorite daughter had eloped with a young man of most trifling character, and utterly unworthy of her. It was also known that the father, through the knowledge of the youth's worthlessness, had forbidden him from visiting the house, and had first requested and then commanded his daughter never to see him again. And yet here she had run away with him.

One will ask, were she and the young man of age? We believe they were, and this gave them a legal right; but what of the Fifth Commandment, which says, "Honor thy father and thy mother"? Then there is a wrong way of doing even a right thing; and further still, there is a right way of doing everything. They did not pursue the correct way. The father had done everything for her, and even now was endeavoring to protect her from future misery; but in her infatuation, the devotion and kindness of a lifetime were forgotten and she fled from her girlhood's home in the night.

One of the most painful experiences of the writer's life was undergone in visiting this parent on the reception of the distressing news. As we approached the home, it looked like a house of death. The mother was prostrated, the younger daughter, with red, swollen eyelids, appeared only a moment and vanished, while a servant silently opened the door and led us without a word into the sitting-room, where the father sat in a large rocking-chair, looking twenty years older than when we had last seen him a few short days before.

He was the soul of courtesy, and arose at once to receive us, and tried to assume his old, pleasant manner, but it was a complete failure and sinking back in his chair with his face buried in his hands he groaned out, "Oh, Brother C., my heart was broken."

In another moment almost, and before we could finish speaking some words of tender sympathy, he recovered his composure, and his face assumed the same stony look which had struck us on entering.

After this the hard, set expression never left him. No matter what was said to him in any way about his great sorrow, the look we have mentioned remained unaltered.

A letter came a few days after the elopement from the daughter begging for forgiveness. He sent it back to her with the words, "As she had made her bed, she must lie upon it." She wrote another, but he returned it unopened. She became sick, and we doubt not mainly from remorse at her own conduct, but he refused to go to her, or allow anyone of the family to visit her. The wife and second daughter begged with tears that she might be forgiven and brought back, but he was inflexible.

Just as he had known and said, the man who married his daughter was trifling and unable to support his wife; and again the family besought that she might be brought home and properly cared for. His reply was that "she had chosen her way, let her walk in it. She had laid down with dogs, and must expect to be afflicted with fleas."

A more miserable man than he was at this time we never knew; for while he would not forgive his daughter he still passionately loved her and was endeavoring to throttle and destroy the affection.

After six or eight months the sad-hearted young wife got better in health for the time being, and moved with her husband to a distant State, where he obtained some kind of humble occupation. The contrast between her cramped comfortless quarters, and poor unnourishing food, with the sweet, glad, well-protected and bountifully provided life of her girlhood made a most heart-breaking contrast.

Still other months rolled by, but the father allowed no letter to be written to her by the family, or received from her. News, however, struggled through in some way that she was in great poverty, and in wretched health.

If pity for her touched his heart, he never expressed it. His own face seemed as if carved out of marble, and his eyes had a burning look of misery in them, as if a hidden flame was consuming his soul, or the undying worm had already commenced its everlasting work of spirit torment.

By and by they heard that the wild, wayward son had drifted into the very neighborhood of his sister. In one of his rare letters he said that "she looked like the wreck of herself."

Still the father gave no sign of yielding.

One day he went down to the village postoffice. Two letters were handed him. One was in the handwriting of his prodigal son. He opened the envelope in front of the office and read the crushing tidings that his daughter, the wife of scarcely twenty months, had just died.

With a face as white as a corpse, and hands shaking as if with an ague, he took up the second letter, which was dated a day later than the other, was addressed in a strange hand, and had the words "In haste" written in one corner. Literally wrenching it open the wretched man read the astounding information, from an utter stranger, that his son, the very one whose letter he had just read, had been instantly killed that same day by the explosion of a steam gin boiler, before which he happened to be standing.

Some in the postoffice heard a loud groan, and then a heavy fall on the pavement outside. Running to the place they found the doubly-bereaved man stretched full length and unconscious on the brick walk, with the two letters grasped in his hand; one announcing the death of the daughter written by the son, and the other telling of the shocking end of the son himself, the very day after he had written the sorrowful news about his sister.

The above sketch is not fiction, but an actual occurrence. Truly we do not need to go to books, or to the drama, to see and hear remarkable and sorrowful things. The darkest tragedies are taking place around us in life all the time. Men and women are continually meeting us on the street, sitting by us in the car and in church, who are actually staggering, fainting, falling and dying under burdens and sorrows that are too great for human strength to bear. The most heartbreaking things do not always appear in the papers; and greatest griefs remain forever unknown.

How pitiful we ought to be to that procession of life constantly filing past us, with loads heavy enough already; and yet to them far sadder things are coming. A yellow envelope marked "Telegram" is delivered, but it proves a lurid lightning bolt to the heart! A letter is received at the postoffice; and it means when opened that the sun of earthly happiness has set forever!

V.

The Restoration of a Preacher

He was a Methodist preacher and had been for years a very useful one. He obtained the Baptism of the Spirit and became much more useful, getting not only his own church blessed, but holding meetings for his ministerial brethren and having gracious revivals on their works wherein many souls received free and full salvation.

The subject of this sketch, whose name was D., had the double gift of writing religious verses or hymns, and composing melodies to wing them on their flight. He collected a number of his own composition and had them published in book form. God honored this little volume of Gospel song, as He had already blessed the ministry of His servant. Among these hymns was one he called "The Prodigal Boy." The chorus ran,

> "But for one far away there remains a place,
> For his father doth love him still;
> And he can come back to his loving embrace,
> Yes, he can come back if he will."

This hymn seemed to be peculiarly honored of heaven. The author scarcely ever sung it without seeing someone leave his sins and backslidings, and come home to God.

By and by something got in between the disciple and his Lord. Then followed a gradual loss of joy and power, later a greater drifting, and at last a heart-sickening distance from the Saviour, which the man perfectly realized in himself and which was equally manifest to others.

What bent led to the commencement of the backsliding is not known. The man may have been betrayed into the habit of scolding, fault-finding, unkind suspicion, and harsh judgment. Many go this way.

He may have unconsciously presumed on the prerogative of the Pope and became infallible. He may have spoken where God has been silent, set up a standard of Christian living according to his own ideas and notions, and insisted that his brethren adopt it or be excommunicated if not actually run out of the ministry and country for nonconformity to his opinions.

It may have been a grosser though not a more hardening sin that led him astray. Anyhow, his face clouded, his voice got rasping, his shouts ended, his songs ceased, his testimony was no more, and soon he was out of the ministry.

News came that he had taken up some kind of secular work, and then had moved to a large city. After that he was lost sight of for several years.

At this time the writer was sent to the same city as the preacher in charge of one of the churches. He was conducting a meeting in his own charge, and had a singer employed to assist him in that part of the work.

One night after the sermon had been preached, the altar call made, and many were coming forward, the leader of song, who was at the organ rendering hymn after hymn of invitation, suddenly saw Brother D., the subject of this sketch, sitting in the back seat of the crowded auditorium. The singer, whose name was R., knew D. and his history well, and seeing him thus suddenly after the lapse of years, felt like one beholding the face of a man looking at him from the crest of a sea wave, who was supposed to be at the bottom of the ocean.

Calling the writer quickly to his side R. told him that D. was present, and where he could be found. After a few moments we turned our eyes in the direction which had been whispered, and saw one of the most melancholy faces we ever beheld. The man had black hair and eyes, and possessed a striking face naturally, but the deep-settled sadness on his countenance would alone have attracted attention in any assembly. It was not simply grief that had left its stamp, but the dull, dead look of a hopeless sorrow.

The initials of the man's name were S. A. D., and if ever we saw a face that measured up perfectly to these initials, it was the countenance of D., the man pointed out to us.

As we were looking at the wanderer, who had been washed up by a billow of God's providence from the great Deep of the world outside and thrown on the strand of our meeting, we noticed that R. was playing the organ with one hand and busily turning over and looking at a number of different song books that were piled up on a shelf in the instrument. At last he seemed to get the one he wanted. Glancing at the title on the back we saw it was a copy of D.'s own song book.

Opening quickly at a certain page, R. deftly placed the book before him and began playing and singing "The Prodigal Boy." We never heard him sing better, and when he came to the chorus he fixed his eyes on D. and fairly poured forth the words:

> "But for one far away there remains a place,
>   For his father doth love him still;
> And he can come back to his loving embrace,
>   Yes, he can come back if he will."

The instant R. began singing the hymn D. gave a sudden start, and cast a look at the singer that was indescribable in its mingled surprise, pain and despair. But R. sang on through each stanza, and reaching the chorus he would repeat it again and again, throwing his very soul into the words, until we saw D.'s head going down, his face buried in his hands and his form shaking violently; when he suddenly arose and, almost staggering up the aisle, fell down at the altar with groans that went to every heart. The song which he had composed and had often sung with the result of bringing sinners and backsliders to salvation, had been used by the Holy Spirit to draw the author himself back to God.

R., with his face shining with joy, left the organ, ran to D., and, throwing his arms around him, wept and prayed aloud a marvelous prayer on his behalf.

D. was reclaimed that night, and before the week ended swept back into the blessing of full salvation. He then joined our church.

In the course of a year the writer gave up the pastorate and became an evangelist. He left a strong Holiness church behind him; but the Great Adversary laid his plans and secured his human abettors to discourage, silence, divide and scatter this wonderful band of sanctified people.

In a return trip to the city, after an absence of a few months, a great change was plainly observable in the church. There was little or no response under preaching. The altar was empty. The prayer meeting preceding the main service at night was thinned out, and had but little glow and vigor. In the testimony service there seemed to be a studied avoidance of the word sanctification.

We were told in explanation that the pastor had requested there should be less noise in the prayer meeting, and that the obnoxious word should not be used, as it was offensive to some church members, and was not understood by still others.

With a closer attention after this side light, we observed that a number of faces we had last seen all ashine with holiness, were now in shadow. With a thrill of pleasure we noticed at the same time that D.'s countenance was far brighter than we had ever seen it.

A later visit showed a greater thinning out in the Holiness ranks. A number had lost the experience and were repossessed of dumb spirits, others had gone elsewhere for spiritual food, and a few had undertaken various kinds of mission work in the city, in a spirit of self-preservation and to feed and rescue souls they saw starving and dying around them.

In the little band left in the church who were still true to Full Salvation we saw the bright, joyous face of D. He seemed to have passed out of the rank of the "thirty" and entered the still higher grade of the "three."

A still later visit to the city brought a crowning wonder. The very individuals whom we expected to keep the Holiness Band together and be leaders and protectors in the time of adversity, had failed to do so. But, lo! at this trying moment D. had come forward and quietly taken the front rank, and was the comforter, counselor, helper and leader of the misunderstood, despised and opposed little company of the sanctified.

This was the last time we saw him. He possessed the respect and confidence of his pastor, enjoyed the love and trust of the Holiness people, and was flourishing under the smile, favor and constant blessings of God.

The curtain, so to speak, drops on him here, for we have not seen him for many months. But he is still true to God, uses his song book, and, above all, possesses the Spirit which makes his talks, prayers and hymns effective.

Among the large number of religious songs he has written, he has not given to the world a sweeter and truer one than "The Prodigal Boy." The chorus alone has in it the sweetness and fullness of the Gospel. Not only many wanderers brought back to God can testify to this, but the author himself of the hymn and chorus can say, I know it is true.

How his heart must swell with love and gratitude as he stands before an audience today and sings:

> "But for one far away there remains a place,
>   For his father doth love him still;
> And he can come back to his loving embrace,
>   Yes, he can come back if he will."

VI.

A Devoted Wife

We have known parents who were tender, sacrificing and devoted to their children, to be rewarded by ingratitude, disobedience, neglect and gross insult. On the other hand, we have seen fathers and mothers who were cold, exacting, selfish and at times cruel to their offspring, who had in return for such unnaturalness as faithful, loving and self-denying children as ever blessed a family circle. Reason, analogy and everything else would have prophesied and expected different results in each case, and yet here were the granite facts before one as described.

Again, we have seen a man who provided well for his household, denied his wife nothing, had not a single offensive habit like tobacco or whisky to make his presence in the house disagreeable, and yet in face of all that, was treated to the day of his death as a mere cipher, or figure-head, in the family. He never knew a whole day of pleasure and happiness in his entire married life.

Remarkable to say, we have beheld the opposite picture, where the man reeked with tobacco, was scarcely ever from under the influence of liquor, was blustering and profane, was insulting and cruel, never made a plan for the pleasure of his household, and fairly ignored the presence of his wife and children; and yet she and they clung to him with an undying affection through everything, and when the poor moral wreck and life failure was in his coffin, the woman flung herself upon the pulseless clay with a heartbroken wail, and was carried to her room unconscious.

Men may try to account for these cases, and give sapient reasons for the remarkable unnatural results, but the facts remain the same after all the learned explanations.

When a lad of twelve we first saw Colonel and Mrs. J., as they were paying a brief visit at the residence of a married sister of the writer. They owned a large and beautiful cotton plantation and were wealthy. They were both brunettes, he about thirty-five years of age and she twenty-eight, and a finer-looking couple it would have been hard to find.

Two things impressed even the careless at once about them; one was that Colonel J. was a dissipated man, while Mrs. J. was perfectly wrapped up in her husband. When he spoke, her ears never lost a word, and when he was not speaking her eyes would dwell upon his face with such an expression of tenderness and fondness that print could not have been plainer. It mattered not what he said or did, whether he noticed her or not, whether he was polite or rude, the beautiful brown eyes of the woman fairly baptized the man with her rich, overflowing affection.

No sun plant ever followed the great orb of the day with a more devoted gaze than this woman attended with unchanging and glorifying love the man of her choice. As some flowers can only live in the sunshine, she seemed only to exist for, and in the presence of her husband. She seemed to be filled with a great inward joy when he was around, and drooped or grew restless when he was absent.

Colonel J. was a fine-looking, dashing Southern gentleman, but was absorbed in himself, and being nearly always under the influence of liquor, had no eyes to observe the devotion of his wife, and if he did, took it as a matter of course.

The steady drinker is compelled at last, through the abuse of brain, nerve, and every other power, to become moody, irritable, and fault-finding. All this naturally came first on the wife; but she bore it without a murmur. Later there were dreadful out-bursts of wrath; and some said, who were best acquainted with the family, that there were acts of physical violence, and that they came upon the body of this faithful woman. If it was so, such a statement never fell from her lips: indeed, at this time she became, if possible, more devoted to her husband.

One day a physician was suddenly summoned to the residence, with the information that Mrs. J. had swooned. The doctor, who was a very observant man, bent over the unconscious woman and saw at once that it was no ordinary fainting spell. His hand was busy searching for contusions and fractures, while Colonel J. paced restlessly up and down the front gallery.

When consciousness was restored the physician asked the sufferer how a certain large bruise came upon her face. She replied without a moment's hesitation that "It was likely she had fallen and inflicted it on herself."

The doctor fixed his gaze steadily upon her and said:

"Mrs. J., has it occurred to you that the boot-heel of Colonel J. made that mark?"

And the woman, with the great, pathetic brown eyes fixed unwaveringly on the doctor, and protecting her idol to the last, said quietly:

"No, sir; it has never so occurred to me."

The physician gave a heavy sigh, left her side, and, walking past Colonel J., on the gallery, refused to speak to him and, mounting his horse, rode away.

A few months after that Colonel J. got into an altercation with the overseer on his plantation, and shot the man down in cold blood. The murderer was at once arrested, brought to the town where the writer lived, and lodged in jail.

Mrs. J. immediately came to the same community, took board at one of the hotels, but spent most of the time with her husband in his dark and unattractive little cell. As the murder was so foul and pitiless, the court refused the prisoner bail.

The trial came on after several months, and dragged its way along for days and weeks. The Colonel had money and made a hard fight for his life. But eloquent and skillful manipulation of the case by able men could not alter the ghastly facts, that a cruel murder had been committed. And so the verdict was brought in one day by the foreman that the prisoner was guilty in the first degree. The Judge put on his black cap, and, looking at the pale man before him, pronounced that on a certain day he should be hung by the neck until he was dead, closing with the usual words, "and may God have mercy on your soul."

At this moment there was the crash of a falling body, and Mrs. J. was carried almost lifeless from the room. All the summer she had stayed by her husband's side in the poorly-lighted and worse ventilated jail; nor had she left him through all the painful scenes and experiences of the court-room; but now, on hearing the words of doom, she seemed unable to bear up another moment, and fell with a breaking heart to the floor.

On being borne to the outer air, she recovered immediately and begged to be led to her husband. With a calmness that impressed all with wonder she went by the doomed man's side to the jail. A number who observed her face that day were struck with a strange resolute look, which gleamed in the eye and declared itself in lines of the countenance, and which they translated into a determination never to leave him again, until he walked upon the scaffold six weeks from that day. How completely they misread that look on her face! And how little they dreamed of the depths of devotion in a woman's heart when she really loves!

At this period the writer saw Mrs. J. a number of times at his sister's house. She still remained a very beautiful woman, but her face was deadly pale, and she had an abstracted expression in her eyes that was altogether unusual. She would have to be spoken to several times on some occasions before she seemed to hear; then would say, "Oh, I didn't hear you. I was thinking of something."

Of course all hearts ached to see her look so, and answer as she did, for we imagined that her thoughts were with her husband in the cell, and anticipating the last dreadful scene on the scaffold.

She visited no one else save our sister, whom she loved very much, and explained even these brief calls by saying that she took this little time from her husband in the way of exercise and recreation, simply to keep up health and strength for his sake. Three or four times she paid hurried visits to her plantation, but would return the same day. As she had left her two little daughters, aged eight and nine years, at the country home, and as her temporal interests naturally demanded her presence on her place once in a while, nothing was thought of these occasional trips.

One afternoon, in saying adieu to the writer's sister, Mrs. J. said "Good-by, dear; I may not see you again."

"Why, where are you going?" cried our sister.

Mrs. J. became crimson and seemed confused; but only for a moment. She replied quietly:

"Oh, nowhere; but in these times when war has commenced, we don't know what will take place."

The very next morning the town was electrified with the news that Colonel J. had escaped from the jail! The sheriff, deputy and possés sworn in as assistants, searched the swamps in every direction, but the rescue and flight had been too well planned and carried out by the devoted wife, and so Colonel J. disappeared forever from his native country and State.

That resolute look on her face that day at Court meant that she was determined that her husband should not hang, but be rescued. So while she visited him, going in and out of the jail, she took the impression of keys and locks upon wax. Her trips to her plantation were to have her own blacksmith make the iron skeletons which were to free her husband. It took several journeys to get them fashioned exactly right. Then she had a faithful servant to station himself with a fleet horse in the edge of the swamp near the town on a certain night. It lacked then only a week to the day of the execution. And it was that afternoon when, in her restlessness, Mrs. J. paid her last visit to the home of our sister as described, and came doubtless to be reassured that there was no suspicion existing as to the proposed break and dash for liberty. From that last visit she went to the jail, sat with her husband until nightfall as usual, gave him the keys, a pistol, and money, and then returned to her room at the hotel.

At midnight, when all was still, Colonel J. quietly unlocked the door of his cell, and then the outer gates with the manufactured keys, went to the edge of the swamp where the faithful negro was awaiting him with a horse, and was forty miles on his way to the Mississippi River before he was missed. He reached the shore, took a steamboat going northward, crossed the lines, and was lost to view of friends and enemies in the South forever.

Mrs. J. retired to her plantation, and became a recluse for months. She may have been waiting for something. Perhaps a message.

Meantime the Civil War raged, and the fleets of the north filled the Mississippi River and her armies penetrated the State. Maybe the summons came then from the absent one; for suddenly Mrs. J. disposed of all her property, and, with her two little girls, took a swift and almost unnoticed departure, got across "the lines" somewhere, and disappeared in the far away North as had done her husband.

We have never heard of him or her since that time. Whether they rejoined each other, and whether they are alive or not, we do not know. We do know, however, that if ever an unworthy man was blessed, enriched and actually glorified by the perfect love of a noble woman, Colonel J. was that man.

We never think of her devotion without recalling a couplet of Tom Moore:

> "As the sunflower turns on her god when he sets,
> The same look which she turned when he rose."

As we also recall the deep melancholy of her face, which had become so through the coldness and unkindness of her husband; and remember how it deepened into a hopeless look, as through the faithlessness of one man the whole world had become black and empty to her; we have thought of still another poem of that same matchless poet of the heart, as he described the despair of a woman whose heart had evidently been broken in an identical way.

This is the last verse,

> "Do I thus haste to hall and bower,
>   Among the gay and bright to shine,
> Or deck my hair with gem or flower,
>   To flatter other eyes than thine?
> Ah, no! with me life's smiles are past,
> Thou hadst the first—thou hast the last."

VII.

A Clerical Fraud

The individual spoken of in this chapter made a sudden appearance at one of the Southern Methodist Conferences, bearing with him the credentials of a traveling preacher of that denomination, and also having in his possession several letters of introduction.

He was a man of about thirty or thirty-five years of age, fairly good-looking, with decided intellectual and oratorical gifts, and having what might be called an ingratiating manner. He seemed desirous of pleasing.

The Bishop took to him at once, and begged of his Cabinet a good appointment for the stranger who was knocking at their gates. He especially desired that he should not be sent to a town in the swamp country, lest his health be injured. Accordingly he was appointed to one of the strongest churches in one of the pleasantest and healthiest cities in the bounds of the Conference.

In taking charge the Rev. Mr. H., who was a widower, as he reported, was boarded in the sumptuous and hospitable home of Mrs. L., a leading and wealthy member of the flock. Mr. H. had with his other luggage a large lady's trunk, filled with the clothing of his deceased partner. Mrs. L. aired the really rich and beautiful garments every few weeks, and as H. would pass along the back gallery and view the dresses, shawls, mantles and other articles strung upon the banisters, he was observed repeatedly to put his handkerchief to his eyes, and seemed nearly overcome. Dead though the wife was, her memory evidently was very precious to the bereaved husband, and his emotion gained him great credit with Mrs. L. and other observers.

In his pastoral and congregational relations Mr. H. took mainly with the old and the young. He made special efforts to win these two classes by grateful attentions to the former, and a delightful friendliness and familiarity with the latter. The middle-aged class of the church did not take to their new pastor. Among them were a number of spiritual people, who said that his sermons were fine but did not reach the soul; that his manners were agreeable, but they left the impression after contact with him, that he was not sincere, and that his politeness was affected or put on.

Meantime the congregation increased, worldly people flocked to hear the brilliant orator, the choir was magnified, much singing talent enlisted, great bunches of roses bedecked the pulpit, and charming entertainments were provided for the young people.

While the elderly members of the church as a rule were delighted with their preacher, there was an exception in the person of old Brother C., who was down on "the whole innovation," as he called it, and was especially sore about the flowers in the pulpit. He said it was an abomination. Of course the preacher had these remarks repeated to him by his special friends.

One Sunday morning Mr. H. met Brother C. in the vestibule. The pastor was loaded down with some clusters of roses and several large bouquets which had just been given him in front of the church. Desiring to speak to some ladies in the porch he turned to Brother C., and, laying the flowers in his hands, begged him in his most bewitching way to please place them on the pulpit for him. The venerable old trustee looked like he had received an electric shock, but grasping the roses in his hands he marched up the aisle and deposited them on the rostrum stand in full view of a most intensely amused congregation. The pastor himself seemed to be bathed in smiles, though Brother C. was not affected one particle in that way. This was patent to all.

The preacher's success in filling the pews, and building up certain social departments of the church drew some of his ministerial brethren to look at his audience and study his methods.

One of these visiting preachers (now a Bishop) was invited to preach. He did so, while H. led in prayer, abounding in striking expressions as he did in his sermons. This time the memorable sentence which the Bishop to this day quotes was, "We thank God that when man went astray, Mercy followed him."

Among the Bishops of the Southern church at the time of which we are writing was one who had a remarkable faculty in scenting sin and discovering impostors. The writer once heard him say he could tell a fraud by his shoes. This badge of guilt, however, was used by him as a corroboratory rather than a primary sign. He refused to explain the telltale feature of the shoes, and will doubtless carry the secret to his grave, as he is now far advanced in years.

Some kind of rumors reached this Bishop, whom we will call X. We do not know but they came from letters of Bishop X himself asking for information about the character of the new preacher's work. Evidently the answer was so unsatisfactory that the Bishop wrote to one of the leading stewards that he was coming up on the next day's train to look into matters. The steward, gratified at the reception of a letter from such a high quarter, told it to his wife, who repeated it to her special friend, who whispered it to her crony, and so it went until, in a few hours, the information came to the ears of H. himself. It was told him on the street by one of his admirers, who saw nothing but a compliment to H. in the episcopal visit.

The news, however, had a very strange effect on H., who instantly became deadly pale, excused himself, looked at his watch, and soon after was seen in a hack driving up the street. A few minutes later he appeared at Mrs. L.'s residence in a very agitated condition, and telling her that he had received distressing tidings calling him away for a while, he departed with his baggage and his dead wife's trunk, leaving Mrs. L. weeping on the front gallery. An hour later the Rev. Mr. H. was on the train with his two trunks, flying northward at the rate of forty miles an hour.

The next day Bishop X. arrived to find his bird flown; while on the northern mail came a letter to a prominent citizen asking if a man answering to H.'s appearance was figuring as a preacher in one of the churches, and stating that the writer of the letter was the wife of H., who had deserted her and carried her trunk away with him.

Of course this was all a great shock to the community, and the cause of Christ was wounded, while the children of God mourned. Many in the church said, "I told you so." Brother C.'s stock went up at once with a bound. Some ardent friends of H. refused to believe a word of the exposure, while Mrs. L., good old soul as she was, made the most remarkable speech of all. Confronting an excited group, she cried out, "What made them find out all this about him; he was doing well and giving perfect satisfaction; why didn't they let him alone?"

As for H., after going northward several hundred miles he took another road and returned south, and twelve or eighteen hours afterward rolled into New Orleans, still a preacher, but this time a Baptist minister. His credentials and letters of introduction all purported that he belonged to that denomination.

In a few days he became pastor of a congregation, began to draw at once, and became the idol of the worldly part of the audience. This time he was a single man, and his name was changed from H. to Copeland.

In two weeks' time the lightning stroke of a sudden, unexpected exposure fell upon him, the papers printed it, and the telegrams flashed the sickening news over the country. Someone who had seen him as H., the Methodist, was stricken all but breathless in listening to him one Sabbath morning as Copeland, the Baptist.

The hunted, unhappy being fled again, boarding a north bound train. The young men in the town which he had deceived as a pseudo Methodist heard he was coming by on the cars and prepared to meet him at the depot with a bucket of tar and bedtick of feathers. But their intended victim had taken the lightning express and passed their station six hours earlier than expected, and so again a richly deserved punishment was escaped.

He next appeared in a Tennessee town as a local preacher, with parchments and all the other necessary papers required to substantiate the claim. He was elected superintendent of the Sunday school, and became engaged to the daughter of a wealthy church member. He succeeded in his deception here just three months, when one of those letters in female handwriting arrived, addressed to the postmaster, asking if a man of H.'s description was there. Before the owner of the trunk could swoop down on the deserting husband, H. learned that the inquiring epistle had arrived, and that the postmaster had replied affirmatively; when the wretched being started to run again. This time the young men of the community, who were indignant at the wrong perpetrated against one of the finest girls in their town, caught the fugitive as he was trying to board a train, and plastered him with such a covering of tar and feathers that his best friend would not have known him.

After that there came a single rumor that he had appeared in a town in Canada, had begun again his work of deceit, when in some way he was found out and he had fled in the night.

These things transpired in 1874 and '75. Since that last flight H. has never been heard of again. Whether God grew weary of him, and took him from the world which he was cursing; or whether in his next effort he succeeded, and is now the acceptable pastor of some town or city church, we do not know. We only know that for twenty-six years he has dropped out of sight and hearing as though he had toppled over the horizon, and fallen from the world into bottomless space.

*   *   *   *   *   *

In reviewing this man's life we have often thought that if his misdirected energies had been projected instead into proper channels he would have been a benediction to countless thousands and caused a multitude to rise up and call him blessed at the last day.

We read of a person who spent twelve hours in making a counterfeit two and a half shilling piece. We also recall hearing of a negro who consumed an entire night in stealing three sticks of wood, when the honest labor of a day would have secured him a cord instead, together with a good night's rest after his toil had ended, and a quiet conscience at that.

So we have thought of H., that if he had devoted half of the time, and part of the skill and force and labor which he was using to deceive people and do wrong, into right directions, he would have been as great a joy and comfort to the church and mankind as he had been a cause of distress, confusion and mortification. If his remarkable force and generalship had gone purely into ecclesiastical channels he would have been elected a Bishop; or if the push, energy and devotion to his purpose of fraud had been run in lines of piety, he would have won the white robe and golden crown of a saint.

VIII.

A Remarkable Conversion

He was a heavy-set man, with square face, beetling brows, keen grey eyes, and complexion bordering upon the florid. There was nothing in the muscular, almost day-laborer appearance to suggest the idea of a first-class intellect lying back undeveloped in the massive and almost shaggy head; and no one would have dreamed that the man possessed a passion for flowers and exquisite taste for paintings of first-class merit, and all real works of art, whether they were the creations of the brush or the chisel.

Along with this ardent love of the beautiful, was a sinful nature that would assert itself at times, and rush on its reckless, thoughtless way with the sweep of a storm or flood.

While still a young man he enlisted in the army at the time of the Mexican War, and under Scott or Taylor marched and fought in that land. Having no fear of God before his eyes he had also no fear of man, and gave a vast deal of trouble to the military authorities. He was a brave soldier, but with cyclonic tendencies and movements toward all restraints of custom or law.

On one occasion he stole away from camp, and scaling the wall of a great Catholic cathedral, broke through one of the lofty windows, and descended inside the sanctuary, having used the head of the apostle Peter as one of his stepping stones downward. As we remember the account, he injured the statue and disarranged its drapery. But to these misdeeds he scarcely gave a thought, as he almost instantly became absorbed in the study of a number of old paintings that hung upon the walls. Hours fled unnoticed by the enraptured man, until he was suddenly discovered by the priests and attendants.

An arrest followed, and later still a trial which had both civil and military features in the way of punishment, and it surely would have gone very hard with the transgressor had not a lady of the nobility exerted her influence in his behalf. Hearing that a common soldier had broken into a cathedral and spent hours in the study of works of art, she insisted that he was no ordinary man, and setting in motion strong influences, secured the soldier's release, and very likely the sparing of his life itself.

All this failed, however, to operate as a check on L.'s wild career. He went onward in the same thoughtless, sinful course, until suddenly a simple, touching circumstance brought about the complete change of his life.

A soldier had died and was being buried, while his company, drawn up in ranks, stood around the grave. As the body was being lowered a small Bible was observed resting on the breast and near the folded hands of the dead man.

L. asked what it meant, and was told that the book was the Bible, and it had belonged to the mother of the soldier; that when he was dying he requested that it should be placed over his heart, and buried with him.

The instant that L. received this simple explanation the tears gushed into his eyes, and he gazed into and at the grave like one fascinated.

After the platoon firing over the freshly made mound, L. marched back to the camp with his comrades, but returned a deeply convicted man. The sight of a Bible on a dead soldier's breast had done the work, when every other effort put forth by earth and heaven had failed.

His sorrow of heart and agony of mind over his sinful life were pitiful and remarkable to behold. One day he borrowed a Bible and plunging into the woods until he came to a remote place, attempted to read the Word. But it seemed a locked volume to him and only added to his torture. With deep groans he rolled upon the ground and cried aloud that he was lost.

At last the idea occurred to him of opening the book at a venture and trusting to find direction and relief through the first verse which met his eyes. He did so and the passage which his distracted gaze fell upon was:

"Ephraim is joined to idols: let him alone."

As L. read what seemed his death sentence he fell again upon the ground with awful groans, feeling that he was a doomed man. But seized with a sudden impulse he took up the open Bible and, placing the verse, "Ephraim is joined to idols: let him alone," directly over his heart, he rolled over on his face and cried out with a wail which rang through the forest, "O Lord, do the best You can for a poor sinner," when instantly salvation rushed into his soul, his burden was gone, and the woods echoed with his shouts and hallelujahs.

When L. returned to his native State, after the close of the Mexican War, he joined the church and entered the ministry. It soon became apparent to his Conference that in the rough-featured itinerant, a preacher had come in their midst of transcendent pulpit ability.

Whenever sent to a new appointment his massive, rather heavy face and careless mode of dressing and eating were decidedly against him, and first opinions were generally unfavorable; but when he entered the pulpit it was like a king taking his throne, and when he came out it was like a general and conqueror fresh from a great victory, loaded down with spoils. The man had glowed like a seraph for an hour, and swept everything before him with a flood of resistless logic and eloquence.

The writer was a young preacher when he first heard this pulpit giant; and to this day recalls the intensely thoughtful face, the flashing eye, the glow of the countenance, a peculiar tremulous note in the voice when at his best, the wealth and aptness of his synonyms, the wonderful fullness of his vocabulary, and, above all, his tremendous power over an audience, which he stirred and swept as a wind would a field of wheat.

Two things we never failed to observe about this man when he was on his feet speaking; one was that the instant he opened his lips people listened; another was that upon all his auditors rested the conviction that the preacher had barely touched the store of his mental and spiritual wealth. He had the unmistakable look and bearing which comes from conscious reserved force. Some speakers sit down after a sermon leaving the impression that they, the audience and the subject itself are all exhausted. But L., after flooding the minds of his hearers with new light and enriching their hearts with treasures from the opened up Word, would conclude, leaving the congregation with the delightful feeling that they had been granted, figuratively and comparatively speaking, just a crossing over the threshold; just an entrance into the hall or upon the first floor; while galleries, corridors, rooms and upper stories remained still for future exploration and possession. '

Many were the sinners he turned to God, and wonderfully did he build up God's people in faith and service. The simple announcement that he was to preach at Conference was sufficient to crowd the church to suffocation, while the one predominant feeling of the assembly, when he closed the Bible after a sermon of an hour and a quarter, was that of regret that he was ceasing to speak.

Whether from overstudy, overwork, or something else unknown to the writer, a peculiar disease attacked L. when in middle life, and in the zenith of his usefulness. His great intellect went under some kind of shadow, a partial blindness fell upon him, and he had to be led about and cared for almost like a child. He could not recognize faces, and did not know loved ones who were nearest and dearest on earth to him. He could not be trusted alone on the street, and could not find his way from one room to another in his own home. The magnificent mind became almost a total wreck, and all who knew, loved and admired him in his palmy and glorious days, could not refrain from tears as they now contemplated him in his helplessness and childlikeness.

There was one thing, however, that remained about him of his former life and power, and which, whenever witnessed, filled all beholders with wonder and praise as well. This strange thing was that the instant the hour of family worship arrived, and the good wife placed the Bible on his knee, the strength of a spiritual Samson seemed to come upon him, and, after fervently quoting a number of Scripture passages, he would kneel down and pour forth a prayer so tender and full of unction, so remarkable in its felicity of expression, so towering in spiritual thought, and so torrent-like in its sweep from him upon others, as to fill the hearers with amazement and delight. Grace asserted itself above all the ruins of Time, as beheld in the mind and body, and behold! the soul was seen to be greater than all. What some thought were dying flashes of a sinking sun, was really the glorious beams of a marvelous morning, whose light was even then peeping over the rim of another and eternal world.

This strange occurrence taught also a most important truth, and that was, that the work wrought by the Almighty on this soul in the forests of Mexico was not only a blessed but a lasting one. When the weeping penitent fell on his face and cried, "O Lord, do the best You can for a poor sinner," that prayer was wonderfully answered.

Such was the character of the divine performance that day in the southern wilderness, that forty years afterward when the mind was shattered and the body swiftly tottering to the tomb, the beautiful blessed work of grace rose victoriously above all, as a lovely banner has been seen floating majestically and triumphantly over a riddled and crumbled wall.

IX.

A Sudden Recovery

He was an itinerant preacher in one of the Southern Conferences. In mentally reviewing his various gifts, talents and general acquisition of knowledge, he began to feel convinced that justice had not been done him in past appointments. Merit of unmistakable character had not been recognized, and reward not bestowed where it was richly deserved.

The more he brooded upon these things, his excellences and abilities, with the failure of the Conference to recognize his worth, and station him where he properly belonged, the more convinced he was of the wrong done him, and the contempt shown for eminent fitness for the best appointment in the State. As there was no contradictory voice within, the preacher, whose name was Richardson, carried the motion or resolution unanimously in the invisible legislative chamber of his soul.

So it was that the brother attended the next session of his Annual Conference fully persuaded of the foregoing facts and highly expectant of a promotion that would thrill himself and stir the whole assembly of preachers.

All went well until the last day of the session, when, to his unutterable amazement, the hero of this sketch was read out by the Bishop to the poorest of the entire list of appointments!

For a time the man could scarcely credit his hearing; but finally rallying himself, he took up his saddlebags, walked out from the church, mounted his horse, and turning the animal's head toward his home that was twenty miles away, jogged down the road a stunned, grieved and indignant man.

After several miles of profound silence he raised his head defiantly in the air and, speaking to himself, said, "I will not go!'

An inner voice said, "What are you going to do? Will you quit preaching when God called you to do so?"

"No," he snapped in reply, "I won't stop preaching. I will go out on an independent line. I will not let a Bishop and Conference treat me in such a way. I'll go home, raise my own corn, meat and potatoes, support myself and preach to the neighbors and colored people."

"But this is not what you vowed to do when you were ordained and taken into full connection in the Conference," whispered the inner voice.

Whereupon Brother Richardson became quite exasperated in spirit, and replied fretfully, "I don't care if it isn't. I will not be humbled and degraded in this way by men. I'll show them that I am independent of the whole business, and will preach more than I ever did before."

"But," insisted the voice, "you solemnly swore you would go where the Bishop sent you, and your failure now to do this has a moral quality about it, and the disobedience savors of transgression."

Full of vexation the rider jerked his horse and cried aloud to his inner tormentor, "I am no Jonah running from preaching. Did I not say I would give the Gospel in full measure to the colored people?"

So the mental battle raged until he reached the gate of his home, passed through, stabled his horse, and, entering the house, threw his saddlebags in a corner and sank with a heavy sigh into a chair.

His wife's first remark, as she saw him, was, "Where did the Conference send us, Mr. Richardson?"

His grum reply was, "Where I'm never going, madam."

"What!" she exclaimed. "Not going to your circuit?"

"No, madam, I have not the least idea of doing so," and forthwith told her of the Hardscrabble appointment so unworthy of him, and his determination not to go, but to remain at home, make his own living, and preach to the colored people.

As he finished his Jeremiad he said, in a plaintive voice, "I am feeling far from well today."

The wife contemplated him silently for a few moments, and then, rising to go about her housework, remarked solemnly, "You had better go to that circuit, Mr. Richardson," and left the gloomy man to his reflections.

His bad feelings increased so rapidly that in a little while he had to lie down on a lounge, where he sent forth a number of sighs and groans.

His wife, passing through the room an hour later, observed his plight, heard his moans, but failed to be impressed with his sickness. Instead of that she dropped the exasperating advice as she walked out, "You had better go to that circuit, Mr. Richardson."

Now all this was very trying to Mr. Richardson, who, miserable in mind, and fancying himself sick, wanted consolation and even anxiety manifested on the part of his wife for himself. If she had come and sat by him, and said he looked badly and rubbed his forehead and said he was wearing himself out and forcing himself into the grave ahead of time, that would have done him a world of good. For many husbands take a peculiar joy in having their wives alarmed about their health.

But Mrs. Richardson would not be alarmed; but moved serenely about here and there through the house in the discharge of her various duties, and allowed her husband to keep up his lonely and restless tumbling on the lounge.

Finally, as she was passing through on one of her trips, he said to her, "Mrs. Richardson, I am a much sicker man than you think."

This appeal so dear to the masculine heart, utterly failed to reach the partner of his joys, who, quickly replying, "You will feel better when you go to that circuit," disappeared from the room.

As night came on Mr. Richardson's sickness and general bad feelings increased. So that nothing would do but a negro boy should be mounted on a horse and sent post haste after a doctor.

Now, there are doctors, and doctors; just as there are preachers, and preachers. We all know the difference and prefer the other class in both professions. The physician thus hastily summoned was most ordinary in every sense of the word. As for diagnostic skill, he had scarcely a particle. So, after listening gravely to Mr. Richardson's groans, feeling his pulse, looking at his tongue and thumping his chest, he pronounced him a very sick man and measured out some white and yellow powders in certain square pieces of white paper with instructions to take during the night. His medical opinion, given before he left, was that Mr. Richardson had a severe heart attack, at which statement the preacher gave another groan.

When the doctor left Mrs. Richardson went to her bedroom and promptly retired.

The next day was spent in groans by the prostrate servant of God, whose mind was filled with pictures of flying Jonahs, deserting Marks, forsaking Demases, not to mention Judas, Ananias, Esau and Cain. The inner voice also was talking incessantly about broken Conference vows, loss of the respect of his brethren, pride getting a fall, and other distressing things.

Late in the afternoon of the second day the wife went through the room of the sick husband with that strangely unconcerned and unalarmed look on her face. If she had just been anxious about him and looked apprehensive, the invalid would have felt better, but instead she acted as if she did not think there was really anything the matter with her liege lord. Worse still, even after he had been suffering over twenty-four hours on his couch, and his groans had filled the house, she on this second afternoon of his misery, remarked, as she walked through the room, "Mr. Richardson, you had better go to that circuit."

This was too much, even for a well man, to bear, so he turned sharply upon her and said, "Mrs. Richardson, I would thank you, please, to attend to your own business."

This was, of course, a very rude speech, and the preacher himself admitted it a year afterward at a great camp meeting, where he told at a testimony service every fact contained in this sketch. He said, with tears in his eyes, "Brethren, I want you to know what a bad fix I got in once, though it is far from pleasant to confess it."

To resume the story: The second night was worse than the first; so that at midnight the negro messenger was dispatched for the doctor on behalf of the tumbling, tossing, groaning patient on the lounge.

At 1 o'clock the physician arrived, and, after another study of the ministerial phenomena before him, he stated gravely to Mrs. Richardson that her husband was a dying man, and would breathe his last before 10 o'clock in the morning. He told her he could do nothing but leave a few powders to partially relieve the preacher's misery, and would come back again in the morning, although he knew he would be dead before he would arrive.

After the doctor left Mrs. Richardson promptly went to bed again in another room, and the afflicted husband was left alone, save for the company of Jonah, Mark, Demas, Ananias, Esau, Cain and Judas Iscariot.

The unhappy man rolled and pitched; told God many times that he would preach to the colored people; that he would make his own living and not be a burden on His providence; that he was tired of being discounted and trampled upon by men in authority, etc., etc., etc.

He heard the clock strike 3, 4 and 5, and still in sleepless misery he sighed, moaned, twisted and turned upon his couch. He wanted to die. He said so aloud in the dark. Evidently he had forgotten the colored people.

Just then the day began to break. Lying on his lounge he saw the first faint beams in the east, when suddenly, in obedience to a sweet, gentle impulse in the heart from the Holy One of Heaven, he rolled off the couch, fell flat upon his face on the floor, and cried with a loud voice, "Lord, I will go to that circuit!"

When instantly the Holy Ghost filled him! He was on his feet in the flash of a second, leaping around the room, laughing, crying, shouting and praising God, and well, perfectly well, transcendently well, from head to heel, and from tip to tip of his entire being.

It was unquestionably a case of Divine Healing of the highest order, and yet it was also a fact that the preacher took some very bitter medicine just before the Lord restored him. The healing, being of the Saviour, no one need be surprised that it was a sudden recovery.

A few minutes after his instantaneous restoration to health, Brother Richardson was in the backyard splitting kindling for the kitchen stove. A little later he was assisting his wife to cook breakfast. At 9 o'clock he had bidden his wife an affectionate farewell, had thrown his saddlebags on his horse, and was mounted with the head of the animal pointed towards Hardscrabble Circuit. At 10 o'clock he was five miles on the road to his new work, when the doctor arrived at the house according to appointment and prophecy, to see the corpse.

X.

The Fat of the Land

She was a bright, chatty girl, living in and for society, when she met the new pastor of the Methodist Church in the town where she resided. He was a good man, and devoted to the work of saving souls, while she had but little of what is called common sense, and not a particle of piety.

Being bright, however, vivacious and good-looking, she exercised some kind of spell over the plodding young man, and in the marriage which followed another one of those melancholy mismatches was made which abound in the marital world. An eagle and a magpie would have been better mated, or an aerolite and a fixed star.

Their characters, tastes, companionships and lives were entirely different. The man wanted the solid and she the froth and foam of life. He loved souls and she preferred bodies. He lived for Christ, the church and the spiritual good of mankind; and she liked ritualism and impressive forms on the Sabbath, and doted on receptions, dinings, concerts and gatherings of all kinds pertaining to the social world. She had a little income of her own of ten dollars a month, and this she loved to use in giving what she called a "tea," in which a most indigestible lobster salad, strong green oolong, and light bread cut into slices of most amazing thinness contributed the main features. What was lacking in solid nourishing food was made up in painted lamps, tinted shades, heavily draped windows, portiered doors, and in a kind of oriental canopy hung over a rickety lounge. Another substitute for food was the rendering of a certain kind of music by some females in a very feeble and quavering manner, but which Mrs. Phipps, the hostess, pronounced "divine."

Mr. Phipps, the preacher, took neither to the "teas," the household draping, nor the home concerts. He tried several of the entertainments to please his wife, but had such a forlorn, far-away look on those elegant occasions, and there was such an intellectual and moral chasm between the friends and companions of his good lady and himself, that he was allowed after several trials to attend to his parochial work, or to labor in his study undisturbed.

After a few years Mr. Phipps was sent to a circuit which consisted of four country appointments, while he secured board for himself and wife in a town not in the bounds of his work. This necessitated the purchase of a horse and buggy, and occasioned long absences from home of the preacher, who drove over the hills, threading the pine forests, and sought out and visited everywhere his humble membership. Many of his people were farmers, a number were lumbermen and woodchoppers, and all were poor. But they all had souls, and their pastor looked at that side of the case, and labored for their salvation lovingly and unweariedly in the face of a thousand physical discomforts.

He slept on hard beds, ate rough fare, walked and rode until his body ached, and braved every kind of weather. But he got near to the people at the family altar, talked religion with them in their corn cribs and by their spinning wheels, prayed by their sick beds, buried their dead, and became the most welcome and honored of guests in hundreds of humble cabin homes.

Meantime the active, out-of-door life, the nutritious though plain fare, the constant work of doing good, all agreed so well with the preacher that he never looked healthier nor felt better in his life. He gained thirty pounds of flesh, while there was a light in his eye and a ring in his voice which operated like a tonic on the hearts of weary-hearted and discouraged people.

At the same time Mrs. Phipps was steadily growing thinner and whiter on her lobster banquets and light-bread frolics. Much of her old-time vivacity now spent itself in moods that were querulous and snappish. The fatter Mr. Phipps became, the leaner she grew; and the more joyful and serene his spirit, the more clouded and difficult to please was her soul.

The day finally came that the sight of the pastor's wife sitting near her husband would at once suggest to the most careless observer the well-known almanac advertisement picture of

"Before and After Taking." One morning she said to him, with brow all puckered and speech acidulous:

"Mr. Phipps, there is just no use in talking. You are leaving me here to starve to death in this boarding house, while you are flying around among your church members and living on the fat of the land."

Such a vision came to Brother Phipps of corn dodgers and hominy as his wife said "the fat of the land" that he broke into a hearty laugh. But the joyous outburst confirmed the now irate lady in her previous impression, and she was more than ever convinced that she had guessed aright.

The incident led to the pastor's requesting his wife to take one of his trips with him, which invitation she readily accepted.

The first few miles was pleasant enough, but when the preacher turned from the main road and penetrated the poorer regions of black-jack and pine-clad hills, where wretched hovels at wide intervals appeared as the only residences, Mrs. Phipps' face began to wear a reflective air.

Brother Phipps seemed to know everybody on the lonely roads and in the humble-looking dwellings. He stopped to exchange a few words with young and old and informed his disgusted wife that a number of the people belonged to his church.

An hour before nightfall the sun began to cast long shadows from the lofty, sighing pine trees, while the whippoorwills commenced their plaintive notes as dusk approached. None of these sights or sounds helped Mrs. Phipps, who by this time was not only tired, but hungry and in the neighborhood of tears.

They finally reached a creek bottom in which was a farm of ten or fifteen acres mainly planted in cotton. In the center of the field was a log cabin with a puncheon gallery and mud chimney, from whose wide mouth a blue smoke was ascending. There was no sign of a gate, but the preacher, putting his hands to his mouth, began to halloo, "Oh, Brother Wills!"

This was repeated several times, when at last a voice was heard far over in the cotton field near the creek, answering "Hee-oh!" Later the tall cotton began to bend hither and thither, and first Brother Wills' head and shoulders and then his entire body emerged at the end of the furrow, and close to the encompassing ten-rail worm fence, common to that country.

Brother Wills' first greeting to the pair as he turned his sun-bronzed face upon them was:

" 'Light."

Brother Phipps, with responsive cheeriness, "lit," shook Brother Wills' hand and helped his wife out of the buggy. That good lady came forth with about as much spring and elasticity as there is in a bag of lead. Leaning on her husband's arm, she whispered:

"Are we to stay in that rail pen up yonder tonight?"

The husband replied under his breath:

"It is the best house in ten miles around. It has two rooms and a gallery."

Meantime Brother Wills, who was in his shirtsleeves, began throwing the fence down, and driving the buggy through the gap. After this the horse was taken out, the vehicle pushed out of sight in the cotton, and the farmer, leading the animal, preceded his guests up a path which wound through the field, with many a curve, to the house. As Brother Phipps stole a glance at his wife on the way, he saw that her face would have won a prize as a model for "Stony Despair."

Reaching the humble dwelling, Brother Wills made many loud and hearty expressions of welcome, bade them come in, take "pot luck" and "help themselves to all in sight."

As they entered the main room of the cabin, Mrs. Wills was revealed sitting in a hide-bottomed chair carding cotton, with a large sunbonnet on her head. She did not rise, but bade her guests in a hearty manner to "come in, take a cheer and make themselves at home." After a half-hour's social chat that for Brother Phipps and Wills would have perished early, Mrs. Wills suddenly laid aside her cotton cards, and with her bonnet still on her head began the preparation of supper.

Mrs. Phipps was faint with hunger and mental worry, but when she was invited to "draw up and help herself," she found she was unable to partake of the food before her. She could not eat fat pork and boiled cabbage; while cornbread was one of her horrors. The bread served up at their evening meal was what is called ash-cake, a hard pone baked in the fireplace. This with some sickly smelling coffee, constituted the banquet.

Poor Mrs. Phipps! The tears fell from her eyes as she pleaded fatigue and loss of appetite, and was allowed to withdraw to a corner by herself, and rest in a straight-backed, hide-bottomed chair.

Meantime Brother Phipps and Brother Wills talked over the prospects of "Mt. Olivet," "Shiloh," "Bethel," and the other churches on the circuit, while the bread and cabbage steadily disappeared.

That night the preacher and his wife were placed to sleep in the small shed room back of the apartment which had already served for parlor, dining-room and kitchen, and was also the bed chamber of Brother and Sister Wills. After an hour of wakeful and intensely thoughtful silence upon the part of Mrs. Phipps, her husband, with none other but a spirit of self-vindication, whispered to her in the dark:

"How do you enjoy the fat of the land?"

Whereupon the angry woman turned her back upon him, and, burying her head in the pillow to deaden the sound, burst into tears.

The breakfast the next morning was like unto the supper of the previous evening. But Mrs. Phipps could not be persuaded to break her fast. Seated in the buggy a few minutes afterward, and asked by her smiling husband if she desired to go still farther on his circuit, she replied with averted eyes and frozen mouth:

"Home as soon as possible."

It required the soothing influence of several lobster festivals and parlor cantatas and recitals before Mrs. Phipps regained her former equanimity. But with the recovery of her lost composure, it was also noticeable that with it had also come an unmistakable change or gain of something.

One effect of the country trip was the unquestionable dropping of the husband out of all wifely thoughts, plans and calculations. He was in a sense with her as though he did not exist.

A second effect was seen in some kind of mental conclusion the woman had reached, which, whether true or false, she accepted as incontrovertible, and now rested upon as a Gibraltar. It was revealed in a kind of set speech which after this she was found of giving on any and all occasions, but especially at one of the salad and green tea banquets. It was to the effect "That as there are monstrosities in nature, so there are men and women born to be coarse in all their tastes and habits. That people drift and gravitate by natural and inevitable law to plain food and uncultured people, if they themselves are ordinary and uncultivated. That persons are always to be found among those who are most similar to them in taste, temperament and character," etc., etc., etc.

Her argument made one's partiality for pork, cabbage and buttermilk to be unquestionable proof of a vulgar nature, while fondness for lettuce and shrimp salad, with oolong tea, declared just as unmistakably the refined, esthetic soul and superior gentleman and gentlewoman. Her reasoning, of course, abased her husband while exalting herself; and, graver still, completely subverted the sacrificial life of Christ, the self-denying labors of Paul, and the faithful work of every true Christian, who is found in the slums and gutters, in dens and brothels, in hard places and poor-paying appointments, laboring with the vilest and most obdurate, for the betterment, the uplifting and the salvation of poor fallen humanity.

Mrs. Phipps still continues to give her little "Teas," terminating them with a "Reading" or a rendering of musical selections where the ordinary ear utterly fails to recognize a ghost of a tune or a shred of melody. Mr. Phipps is still visiting the sick and hunting up and relieving the poor. Mrs. Phipps has solved, to her own obvious satisfaction, a great problem of life. Anyhow, she thinks she has done so. Meantime Mr. Phipps has a much greater problem on hand. It has never been solved, according to latest reports. His problem is Mrs. Phipps.

XI

He Took the Wrong Road

In the tangled mazes of a Southern swamp it is a grave thing to take what is called the wrong road. Even in thickly settled communities such a mistake means great inconvenience and delay, but when a like blunder is made in a wilderness abounding in impenetrable canebrakes, and crossed in every direction with dangerous sloughs, a much more serious state of things exists, involving not only loss of bearing, but increasing bewilderment, a night in the woods, and even loss of life itself.

In the realm of character or in the way of salvation the "taking the wrong road" is necessarily far more perilous and disastrous. It means, in the beginning, that a wrong moral choice or decision has been made, which, if persisted in, brings spiritual ruin on earth, and the final damnation of the soul in hell. Some have escaped the last woe "as by fire," but whole years had been lost, the reputation hurt, the influence damaged, the character injured and the life itself blighted and blasted by the entrance upon and pursuit of a wrong course of action.

We were attending a large camp meeting located in the piney woods in the South when we first met the person about whom this sketch was written. The writer was a young preacher, and was appointed one afternoon to preach. The text was a double one, "Go thy way for this time"—"Depart from me." The first thought presented was in reference to the peculiar power possessed by the soul to shut God out of the heart and life and keep Him out. The second point made was relative to a retribution suggested by the text and that was confirmed by the Bible, history and individual experience. We were treated in life as we had done to others, and God dealt with us as we had acted toward Him. If we said, "Go thy way" to Him and His messengers, we could fully expect to hear the Judge say at last, "Depart from Me."

We remember in dwelling upon the human side of Retribution to have mentioned several remarkable occurrences of our own personal knowledge that greatly solemnized the audience.

Fully fifty to sixty preachers were present, and among them one who was the acknowledged leader of his Conference. He was invariably sent to the best appointments, and had been elected to the General Conference. To the young preacher's surprise, this prominent minister, whom we will call Dr. Graves, took him aside after the service, and sitting together on a log in the edge of the woods, asked him, after some random remarks, whether he really believed that we were made to suffer as we had caused others; and that events of an identical nature came back in punishment upon us.

We were surprised, not so much at the question as at the troubled appearance of the man. The anxious and even suffering look he turned upon us made a deep impression then, but not as much as it did in after years, when other things threw a stronger and explanatory light upon the occurrence. The fact that a much older and very prominent minister should be speaking with us about the sermon and its effect upon his mind and heart, naturally prevented that closer observation which would have been given under other circumstances. The reply given to him was exactly in the line of the discourse, that we were treated in this world exactly as we had dealt with others. That it was both justice and mercy combined that this should be so in the providence of God. That the lesson was to make us consider the rights, feelings and happiness of others. That it opened our eyes to consider other people as well as ourselves; and we would never know how we had made people suffer until we had been crushed in a similar manner.

We felt in talking that we could not be giving light and knowledge to the distinguished man before us, but he most skillfully drew us out, until having fortified our position with Bible instances and some awful transactions we had personally known, we became more than ever aware of his gloomy looks, and ceased to speak.

Someone called to him at this moment, and he left with a "Good afternoon" and a grating laugh that we have never forgotten.

A year subsequent to this we met again, accidentally, in the office of a merchant. This last-named business man was so profane that the writer abruptly quitted the store and remained on the pavement until Dr. Graves rejoined him. We said in explanation of our hasty departure that we made it a rule to withdraw at once from the company of a man who would take the name of God in vain in our presence.

Dr. Graves, who had given uneasy laughs in the presence of the swearer, said in reply to the writer, "That the early Methodists used to act in the same manner."

Several years after this Dr. Graves preached one night before a large assembly of preachers from the text, "Oh, that my people had hearkened unto me, and Israel had walked in my ways." It was one of the driest, hardest and most hollow-sounding sermons we ever heard. It had not one particle of unction about it, and fell flat and dead upon the congregation.

Two years later a gentleman of high Christian standing told the writer that Dr. Graves had come to his office in great trouble of mind, and said that he wanted to confess something; but receiving no encouragement from him, he had departed without doing so.

Ten years later still, the writer, having become an evangelist, was invited by Dr. Graves to hold a meeting in his church. The city was far distant, but we accepted the call, and opened the battle.

In a few days it was apparent to all that the pastor was in great mental or spiritual distress. Guessing the cause, we preached one night on the necessity of confession, and the advisability of taking a whole night for prayer. We argued that just as some things would not be cast out of us except by fasting and prayer, so there were certain spiritual victories that would never come without a mighty and protracted struggle; that the ordinary, everyday supplication of a minute would not answer; that it would require a Jacob-like wrestle running through an entire night.

Dr. Graves heard the statement, and without consultation with anyone, acted upon it. He spent the night in prayer.

Next morning, as the writer and his singer were walking up the street together, Dr. Graves passed them in his buggy. His appearance was simply shocking. His face had a ghastly, yellowish hue, his cheeks were sunken, and dark rings were about his eyes. The look was that of a corpse. If the Doctor saw us, he never showed any recognition. We were especially struck with the hard, set expression of the man's mouth.

As he passed down the street out of sight, we said to the gentleman by our side:

"He will not make that confession."

He replied, "What do you mean?"

We answered, "He has had his fight last night and did not get the victory. He met the duty of confession face to face, counted the cost of obtaining the blessing of holiness, and has concluded that it was too much, that he cannot afford to pay it."

At the morning meeting Dr. Graves appeared with a large theological work under his arm. During testimony, instead of witnessing to the grace of God as did others, he stood up, opened his volume, and read some passages adverse to the doctrine we had been preaching and to the experience his own people were receiving.

After that Dr. Graves developed into what is called "A Holiness Fighter." He engaged in endless, bitter controversies, and stooped to loud-voiced street arguments against the blessing. He not only preached against it, but would tell the advocates and professors of the experience that they did not have it, and accompany his speeches with a grinding, grating and insulting kind of laughter that was most painful to hear.

Of course this conduct is not surprising to the one who knows and studies the human heart. If Holiness is true, a man must either obtain it or find reasons for fighting it. It will not do to say that we believe in it, and not seek it. On the other hand, if this great grace of God demands of the soul a complete surrender, a perfect humiliation of self for its obtainment, and that soul in a public place or high position cannot get its consent to pay such a bitter price, while friends, acquaintances and congregation are looking on at the struggle, what is left such a person but to fall back on some musty old volume of theology, give a flat denial to the blessing and take up arms from that moment against the religious movement itself? This explains the attitude of many today who spare not the doctrine of sanctification with tongue or pen.

As the years went by, Dr. Graves' frenzy seemed to increase against sanctified people, and he did his best to destroy their work and prevent their holding meetings where his jurisdiction extended.

One of the last letters he wrote was to the writer, warning and forbidding him to hold a Holiness camp meeting in a tabernacle that had been erected within his pastoral limits, or boundaries.

The people pulled up the tabernacle stakes and reared and dedicated the building in the circuit lines of a preacher who promised them protection, and the meeting was held. God came down and many souls were saved and sanctified.

Yet still the man raged on. He even tried to have a revival. But only a handful came out to hear him, the church was dark, cold and empty, and the meeting ended, as it began, without any life, and was felt by everybody to be a flat failure.

Meantime a few of the Holiness people let slip from their tongues a heart-sickening prophecy. The speech finally reached the ears of Dr. Graves. It seemed to exasperate him. A few days later, while in attendance upon the annual convention of his church, he said openly on the streets of the town:

"The Holiness people say that God is going to take my life very soon. Ha! ha! ha!" he laughed, while striking his breast, "I never felt healthier or stronger in my life!"

Within a month's time he was in his grave!

He took the wrong road early in life, and though God in mercy brought him to fork after fork where choosing aright he might have recovered himself and gotten back to duty and happiness, yet, with a persistency that was amazing and horrifying, he would invariably decide against conscience, the Gospel teaching and the strivings of the Holy Spirit; and so taking the way that was not right, followed a course which led him continually farther and farther from God.

His friends erected a tombstone over him, and carved upon it a flattering epitaph. But the sentence that many felt would have best described his life is to be found in the caption of this chapter:

"He took the wrong road!"

XII.

A Sketch of a Child

Among the nations of the earth there is to be found another, whose citizens, while dwelling in every country, speaking the language and keeping the laws of the land, yet remain not the less a distinct and peculiar people.

This nation is a commonwealth of sufferers! It is a multitude of individuals, male and female, young and old, that by the inheritance of some mental or physical malady, or by some accident, or through the power of a desperate sickness in time of childhood, have been smitten, wounded and marked for life. It is a company that by no fault of its own has been ruled out forever from the active pursuits of the world, and shut in to an existence of painfulness, helplessness and loneliness.

There are few families that have not one of these bruised ones of earth; and we have observed that there is a peculiar love and tenderness felt for, and special watchfulness extended over, the little unfortunate who may be afflicted in mind, lame or sightless, or doomed to perpetual silence.

Very beautiful and pathetic have been sights of this character beheld by the writer. One was that of a little girl who, banished from the world lying all around her by some physical affliction would sit upon the floor and lean her head against the knee of her mother for an hour at a time. The mother on one occasion was attending some of our Gospel meetings, and her eyes full of love but shadowed with a wistful, sorrowful expression would often rest upon the child, while her hand, as she listened to the word of God, would wander with a gentle, lingering touch to fondle the nestling head by her side.

Another scene comes to the mind which was beheld many times on the gallery and in the front yard of a neighbor. The gentleman referred to had a child who had some spinal affection, and which required that she should be kept strapped on a plank. Here she would lie not only at night but all through the day; and as the family could not afford a servant, the child did not have the ministry of a nurse, and so of necessity remained in one trying position through the long hours, watching the busy mother and waiting for the evening to come when the father would return home.

The devotion between the two was remarkable; he a great strong man, and she a little helpless mite. How her pale face would light up, and how his would glow and his eyes fill as the poor tired arms would reach up, entwine his neck and the form nestle against his bosom as much as the hard stiff board would allow. He was an overworked man, and came home tired and with dragging steps, but the sight of the tiny sufferer on the plank would act like an elixir and inspiration to him. In another minute we would see him pacing the gallery with his precious burden in his arms that she might breathe the fresh air, or walking about under the trees that she might hear and see the children at play on the pavement, listen to the birds, watch the stirring leaves and catch a glimpse of the quiet beauty of the twilight sky.

In both of these instances we could but notice as we have in many other cases before and since, how these little sufferers are crowned and sceptered monarchs in their way. Their rule is wonderful in its sweep and power. Before them selfishness has to depart, while the better, purer, nobler emotions and powers of the soul are awakened and developed in the highest degree. They are a nation with a mission to other nations. Their reign, if accepted, is one of benediction to the individual, the family circle and to the human race.

$$*\quad *\quad *\quad *\quad *\quad *$$

Marguerite was the baby in the family, and the loveliest of those that had preceded her. When she was still in arms her beauty was widely commented on, and many were the remarks made about her smile, which when overspreading her face, made it one of unusual fascination and power.

At the age of six months through a misstep of one who was carrying her along a dark hall, both fell, and the child received a violent blow on the head against a hard cemented wall. There was, of course, the expected weeping upon the part of the baby, but she was soon comforted and the circumstance of the fall forgotten; when in a few days it was noticed by an anxious-eyed observer in the household that the little one was carrying her head strangely; that the chin was slightly upraised and the back of the head drawn backward.

Two skillful physicians were at once called in, and both pooh-poohed the anxieties and fears of the family away, and easy breaths were once more drawn. But, alas for the superficial knowledge possessed by the most celebrated medical men concerning this profound mystery, the human body. In a week's time the child was stricken down with cerebro-spinal meningitis, and her life despaired of. The first physicians of the city attended the case, a nurse was secured, while the sorrowful-faced young mother would hardly consent to be relieved a minute day or night of the precious suffering burden on her lap.

Great and prolonged was the battle for the life of the little one, and for weeks Death was felt to be not only at the door, but in the room. The fearful experiences of those hours, the anxious and grief-stricken faces of the home circle, the grave look of the doctor, the tossings and sighings of the baby, the periodic clink of the spoon and glass, the low voiced directions of the physician, the stifled sob in the sick room, the sound of weeping from a distant part of the house, and the muffled noise through closed doors and windows of the street outside, all weave themselves into a memory so full of anguish that to this day, after the flight of ten years and more, there are those who cannot bear to summon it back. Like portraits whose faces break the heart to look upon—this recollection or life picture has been turned to the wall.

Finally, when all hope was gone, and the last breath was expected every moment; the crisis was past, and to the amazement and joy of physician, nurse and family, Marguerite lived! But even while tears of thankfulness were pouring down the cheeks of the home circle, it was discovered that the child had become sightless. She was blind. The beautiful brown eyes saw nothing that was held up or moved before them. Then, as the days rolled by, other powers were discovered to be gone. Here was bitter sorrow coming right on the heels of joy; and the thought with many friends was, would it not have been better far for her to have died?

The family moved away to spend the summer on the seashore. It was hoped the sweet, pure, invigorating air of the ocean would help the little one to get back to health and strength. A cottage was secured in Bay St. Louis; and an old French nurse employed to give special attention to the afflicted and all the more beloved child. The two soon became a familiar spectacle to the residents of the well-known summer resort. Sometimes the turbaned creole would croon her old French and Spanish songs for hours on the porch that was shaded by great live oaks and rustling magnolias; the child meanwhile lying on her lap almost without motion, but with her hazel eyes open and evidently listening to every note.

Later in the day the nurse would trundle the sightless, silent listener in her carriage along the beautiful beach, where the only sound heard would be that of the solemn wash and roll of the blue waves of the Gulf of Mexico, as they swept far up the strand, would retire with something like a sigh, and rush back again with their deep-toned and melancholy fall upon the shore.

The child seemed to drink in everything of sound, from plaintive ditties, crooning melodies, woodland bird songs, to the murmur and call of the ocean whose billows rolled and broke near the wheels of her carriage. At this time the breadth of the ocean stretched between the child and her father, though no distance kept her out of his mind.

After this the family removed to a large city in the North to live, and then the long silent child began to sing. With a most remarkable silvery and melodious voice she would pour out for minutes and sometimes an hour that which had been gathering in the line of harmony in her mind and heart. The strains of the old songs sung in the South to her welled up and out, and there seemed to be touching and tingeing them something she had heard from the birds in the woodland and the waves on the shore.

In addition she seemed ever anxious to hear more, and would lie in her carriage in the parlor, or on the lap of a loved one, listening eagerly to the street ballads and songs, and other musical pieces played and sung by her grown sisters on the piano.

It was amazing to see how rapidly she learned anything that had melody in it; and though only eighteen months to two years of age, her voice not only filled but thrilled the house with a loud, clear, accurate and sweet rendition of all she heard. It was a bird-like voice that penetrated every room, and was all the more affecting as she could not speak a word. It was simply a strain of music she poured forth upon delighted and yet deeply touched hearers.

When out on the street in her carriage, escorted by her nurse, it was the same. Lying all helpless, with the pathetic brown eyes open, but seeing nothing, she would sing as we have heard the mocking-birds trill at night in the South. She sang as if her little heart was full, while the clear, child-like voice was easily heard one and two blocks away. It was a medley concert she gave, with "Comrades," "Two Little Girls in Blue," "Marguerite," and "Sweet Marie," together with old French songs that no one knew but the Creole nurse left down South. But everyone was delighted just the same, and many eyes filled as they looked down in the beautiful, sightless eyes, and heard the wondrously sweet melody coming out of the lips of the tiny sufferer—one of that mystic band of God's bruised ones.

Soon after this period the child began to recover her sight, and later to talk. As vision, speech and other powers were thus restored and exercised, strange to say, the sweet, weird and pathetic singing became infrequent, and finally ceased. It was all in vain to coax and plead; a sudden shyness had come, and the home songbird stopped its beautiful notes. Perhaps speech, sight, motion, and other enjoyments relieved the burdened soul, which thus found expression in other ways than in song, but whatever was the cause, the caroling that so charmed the family and many others ended.

As the years slipped by other effects of the dreadful sickness passed away, but it placed the child at the disadvantage of being fully two years behind other children of her own age. With this came a certain kind of timidity, a fearfulness of loud and bold sports, a shrinking from all such play in which she felt herself not the equal in fleetness and strength with her younger sister and other girl playmates.

This led to her retirement from many of childhood's happy games; and to one of the most pathetic of spectacles; namely, the sight of her little figure sitting aloof, watching the children romping at a distance with an indescribably wistful look in her shadowy eyes and resting upon her thoughtful face. Sometimes, on a cold day, when she could not brave the snow and wind outside, she has frequently been seen perched on a window seat, peering through the panes at the laughing, frolicsome set of boys and girls in the yard and on the street and with that same longing melancholy look that made the heart of the observer fairly ache to see.

When thus found by someone of the family in the lonely window nook, she would bury her face in the sympathetic bosom of the mother, father or grandmother, without tears, but with a sigh that went through the very soul of the hearer. She was bowing to the blow of a cruel sickness which she did not remember, but whose sorrowful effect she still languished under. It had struck her backwards two years of time. It had weakened the limbs, made timid the nature, and caused her to be an exile from the ranks of children of her own age, and banished her in some respects from all of them.

*   *   *   *   *   *

Among the stray, cast-off, forlorn animals that tried to insinuate themselves into household relations at the home of Marguerite was a most dejected looking little dog, whose very appearance suggested to most people the thought and desire of administering a kick, letting fly a brickbat, or vociferating the words, "Get out."

The dog was a small one, of a brownish muddy color, while his hair of various length seemed to stand out at every angle. One of his ears had a flop or a droop as if bitten or cut in some way. He had numerous marks of scalds and burns, with deeper scars that spoke of more dangerous weapons than a pan of hot water. The dog bore a wary, frightened look, shambled along sideways, as if watching all points of the compass, and seemed ready to run at the first faintest signal of danger. It would be hard to imagine a more pitiable object in the canine world than the animal now referred to, who made surreptitious visits to Marguerite's home in the wild hope that he might be tolerated if not adopted by the family.

Of course he received prompt invitations to leave, and broomstick handles and other domestic implements were brought into immediate use to hasten his departure. With a pitiful, despairing yelp he would vanish down the street or alley, only to be seen soon after peeping in at the side gate toward the brick kitchen, or wistfully gazing through the iron fence which skirted the grass-covered yard, where the children romped and frolicked in the shade. It all seemed like Heaven to "Sport" as the children of the family for some reason had dubbed the dog. Poor, friendless, homeless, hungry creature, he had no sport, and the principal business of his life was to escape missiles of every kind, as, driven by the pangs of starvation, he crept in at back and side gates in hope of finding a bone, or crust of bread. Poor, smitten and chased roamer of the street, life was nothing but a hard, painful, bitter existence to him.

Strange to say, the first one of the entire household, whose heart opened to receive Sport was Marguerite. No one else could tolerate the ugly, dirty-looking waif of the back alley. It was noticed that her voice had only kind words and tones for him, and her hand was one that slipped pieces of bread to him, secured from the table when the meal was over. The bruised creature of the street found his truest friend in the bruised child of the home which he tried to get into and in vain.

No one relaxed toward Sport like Marguerite. The appearance of the dog was so against him that, after the flight of weeks, the resistance of the household was as firm toward him as at the first. At the same time it was perceived that every time he was ordered off, or kicked out, the face of the child was clouded, and a greatly troubled look gathered in her eyes.

One afternoon the father of Marguerite came suddenly around the side of the house and beheld a scene in the corner of the yard that not only profoundly affected him then, but has remained ever since, a picture in the mind that for pathetic beauty and heart-melting power he has never seen surpassed.

Marguerite was sitting on the grass close to the iron fence, while Sport, with his body lying on the pavement outside, had pushed his head through the metal rods and bars and had it resting on the lap of the child. She was bending over the half-starved, lonely, despised creature, patting his head and smoothing his scarred back, with her fair little hand. He, evidently full of an humble thankfulness, was receiving the greatest act of pity, kindness and love of his beaten and wretched life. The poor, friendless animal, bruised by the hands of men, was being comforted by a little child who had been bruised under the Providence of God.

There was an instantaneous gush of tears to the eyes of the observer, and a swell and ache filled his heart that he had then, and still has no words to describe. He stole away from the spot unobserved, feeling that he had looked upon a scene which had divine beauty in it, and that he had walked upon holy ground.

Since then it has been easier with him to see how and why the sorrowing ones of earth come to the Man of Sorrows; why the stricken and wounded of earth creep up to and lay their wearied heads and broken hearts in the lap of Jesus, who was smitten and hurt all His life, and at last put to a cruel death. There is a peculiar understanding among sufferers. The Bible calls it a "fellowship." Anyhow we know that the bruised One of Mt. Calvary will never cast off the bruised ones of this earth. He bids the lonely, heartsick man or woman draw near to Him. And coming to Him they will find a heavenly lap, where they can weep out every sorrow, feel a tender, pitiful face bent over them, while a hand with a nail print in the palm will with its loving touch lift every burden, remove every pain and fill the soul with a sweet, holy, restful joy which no human force and influence can give and no earthly power can take away.

XIII.

A Brand Plucked From the Burning

Occurrences are continually taking place in the moral world that so break into and over what we call rules and laws in the spiritual life, and so upset certain standards of judgment, that we are for a while left almost breathless, and even after that for quite a season are disposed to be chary of our ex-cathedra utterances upon human life and its destiny, and are willing to allow God to run the world and manage the church and the nations for at least several months.

When we see and hear of people whom everybody thought established in the Christian life, going off into false doctrines, into various evil habits and into sin and unbelief itself; one of those wondering occasions is at once beheld. Great is the clatter and chatter of tongues for a while. The argument of an establishing grace seems to be knocked down. The increased power of resistance to evil said to come from the practice of righteousness appears for a period to be a mistaken idea. And so men are bewildered.

On the other hand, when we see a man who has lived a profane, impure, lawless, godless life for forty or fifty years, suddenly turn to Christ, get saved and then sanctified, and live like a saint, die in triumph and go shouting home to glory, another moral wonder has taken place, and another set of laws, oracular utterances and solemn prophecies have been upset.

The devil of course is around to put his interpretation on both occurrences, and get people to buy his commentaries on all such happenings; and yet the principles by which the two sets of laws were established are perfectly true, and what we see are only exceptions to the rule. In establishing our standards of judgment we simply failed to allow for the presence and power of an

Almighty God not only in the world but in each life, and One perfectly able, with His knowledge of the heart and His omnipotence in this world, to amaze us with the dealings of His permissive and positive Providence.

Moreover, none of these startling things in the spiritual life about us, but have been already spoken of, and fearfully and wonderfully illustrated in the Bible. The Dying Thief was snatched from the lowest step of Ruin and caught up into Heaven. On the other hand, Saul, Judas, and Demas, when well up the stairway of Salvation, stumbled, slipped and fell with a crash to the bottom of an endless Perdition.

So Satan it seems steals messengers of light from the si.e of the Lord, while in blessed contrast the Lord plucks brands from the devil's burning, and transforms them into great fixed stars of righteousness and truth, to shine forever in the heavenly world.

The sketch we here present is a gracious instance of the goodness and power of God in the latter case.

A man named S— was a steamboat mate on the Missouri River. No one ever remembered to have seen him at a church, or heard of his attending one. Moreover, there was nothing about his life to lead one to suppose that he ever had a religious thought, or suspected that he possessed a soul. At the age of sixty-five he was as wicked a man as ever stormed and swore at a set of hands on the deck of a steamboat.

One day while the boat was approaching St. Louis on a homeward trip, he, without a single premonitory sign, was stricken down with that lightning flash and thunderbolt of diseases—paralysis. No one thought he would live through the remaining hundred miles of the trip, nor did he expect anything but immediate death. He heard, as it were, the clods falling on his coffin lid, and expected that the bottom of his grave would next break through and let him slide or plunge into hell.

On arrival at the wharf a litter was made and four men trudged through the silent, empty streets toward his home.

From the moment he fell on the deck, and with every step of his litter bearers, S— was praying to God for mercy. His constant cry was, "Forgive me, Lord, for the sake of Jesus Christ." Before he reached his house, twenty or more blocks from the river, God spoke peace to the tortured soul, and S— was laid upon his bed in his room a saved man.

Some ladies, belonging to the church of the writer, who did a good deal of visiting among the sick, heard of the case and called upon the sick man. In the midst of their visit they happened to speak of sanctification, when, quick as a flash, S— asked what they meant by sanctification; and they replied that it was a beautiful, blessed Grace that God had for His children.

"What!" said S—; "is there anything else?"

"Yes," they answered, "a second work that purifies the soul and fills it with rest and perfect love."

Turning a pair of wistful, pleading eyes upon them, the gray-haired man said, with a broken voice, "I want it; tell me how to get it."

They, however, did not feel competent to give directions, but said they would send their pastor to call on him and show him the way.

The writer, however, was so busy with the numerous and different calls of a city pastorate, that he did not reach the home of S— until the tenth day; when, on entering, he found to his surprise and pleasure that the sick man had obtained the blessing alone, without any more human assistance. Asking the rejoicing person lying before us how he did and what he did to secure "The Pearl of Great Price," he said, with smiles and tears intermingled:

"I wanted it so bad that I couldn't wait. So I kept saying, 'Lord, please give it to me.' Hour after hour for eight days and nights, with every waking moment I would lie here, look up and say, 'Lord, please, for Jesus' sake, give it to me,' and one day, while I was sighing and crying and pleading, the blessing came and I have been full and overflowing ever since. O, yes, I've got it; there's no doubt about it."

As the writer stood by the sick bed of this old river man, one who had not attended church, knew nothing of theology, and had spent his life amid hard and sinful men, and yet was here in the possession of a blessing that bishops are denying and theologians wrangling about, he was filled with such a tide of contending emotions of wonder and awe of God, and love and praise of God, that words could not properly and satisfyingly describe.

We doubt not that the man prayed himself to the point of a complete consecration, and we all know that from the end of such a rod will bloom and bud the flower of a perfect faith in God to cleanse the heart from all sin and fill the soul with the Holy Ghost.

Thus, without preachers, sermons, and altar rails, Brother S—, a poor, ignorant steamboat mate, looking to Jesus, and led by the Spirit, crossed the Jordan and entered the Canaan of Full Salvation, or Perfect Love.

After this it became a crowning wonder to visit him. From the hour of his sanctification until his death, six months later, there never seemed to be a cloud in his sky. His joy was not only like an artesian well, but overflowed everything, and everybody. It was a benediction simply to look upon the shining face of the man, and a privilege to listen to his conversations, or, rather, monologues, for one had only to be with Brother S— a minute to be perfectly willing that he should do all the talking.

We were not only surprised but amazed as we listened to the beautiful, blessed things that fell from the lips of the patient and rejoicing sufferer. As we remembered the churchless and sinful life, we marveled at the man's spiritual knowledge. Where did he get all these gracious thoughts that overflowed in such apt and unctuous language? was the constant query of the mind. And the only answer was that here was a man who had been emptied and filled and was now taught of God.

In the beginning of our pastoral attentions we went down to cheer and help the poor old brother, as we called him. But on the very first visit the tables were turned on us. The invalid helped the well man. The gray-haired man we called on had the youth and freshness of Heaven in him. Instead of being poor, he was

richer in faith, love, joy and other heavenly treasures than any
one of us who entered his sick room. He was a blessing to everybody who called upon him, and the feeling of the visitor at
departure was, that one of the windows of Heaven had been
opened just above that sick bed, and an angel had been met
unawares.

More than once we caught some of our faltering, fainting
members with guile, as the apostle expresses it, by asking them
to drop in and see "poor old Brother S—," who was lying in his
room awaiting the second stroke of paralysis to call him home.
They always came back open-mouthed and open-eyed, full of
wonder and praise, and with their own faith stimulated and
Christian life strengthened at the miracle of grace they had just
beheld.

The second visit of the mysterious disease came as was
expected. It found Brother S— not only prepared but yearning to
depart and to be with Christ. The first stroke found him a sinner
and bade him prepare to meet his God; the second blow knocked
down the door that separates earth from Heaven, and Brother
S— justified, sanctified, exulting and triumphant! walked
through the open portal, and looked upon the face of his
Redeemer.

XIV.

The Fall of Pride

One of the remarkable ways of the world is to judge some sins with the greatest severity and pitilessness, and with the same mouth condone, apologize for, and even exalt other iniquities that will as certainly damn the soul in hell.

Theft, murder and adultery will put a man at once outside social and ecclesiastical pales, while pride is tolerated, cherished and defended; and yet the Bible informs us that by pride fell the angels, and through the like sin Adam and Eve lost the Garden of Eden. They desired to eat the fruit of the forbidden tree that they might be wise and be as gods. In another place is the statement that God knoweth the proud afar off; and still more fearful is the verse that "Pride goeth before destruction, and a haughty spirit before a fall."

This pride may take many forms; of birth, family, position, wealth, culture, accomplishments, beauty and intellect, and can even flourish where there is no reason whatever for its existence except sin in the heart. But no matter whether it is the rebellious will which holds out against God and resists His demands for the humbling of self, or whether it is the haughty spirit which despises the ignorant and poor; all pride is hateful and abominable to God.

The face and hand of the Almighty is against such a spirit and life, and hence it is that the Bible abounds in records of the downfalls of this sin; and in history God is still seen in His Providence, intent upon its humiliation, judgment and destruction. Even in daily life the irony of circumstance, the exposure of accident, the unmistakable retribution of human events, and the direct dealings of Heaven, all agree and point to the fact that pride is certain to meet with crushing downfalls.

In one of our Southern States before the Civil War lived a very wealthy planter, who owned one of the largest sugar plantations in that part of the country called the Coast. He had but one child, a handsome, black-eyed girl, who was eight years of age when the writer first saw her. We met at the home of a relative, where she and her mother were spending the day.

The child, as the heiress of an immense estate, and possessed of great personal beauty, had been much flattered and petted, and so became badly spoiled. She carried, even at that early period of life, an authoritative, not to say arrogant air, and assumed the manner of one of the queens of the earth.

The writer, who was the same age as herself, had the misfortune that morning to offend her majesty in some way; whereupon she flashed upon him such a pair of indignant and angry eyes that the lad, overwhelmed, went down ingloriously before her, and actually crept under a large center table where a heavy cloth covering almost touching the floor hid him from her view. She walked around the captive boy several times in a triumph of spirit, which he felt, or imagined he felt, clear through the heavy drapery which concealed him. Finally she said, in a sovereign-like tone:

"You can come out now; I forgive you."

And the lad, profoundly humbled, came forth to light and life again. The queen, or empress, was disposed to be gracious but the captive was disgusted with royalty and left the little virago the monarch and solitary possessor of the empty room.

A few weeks afterward the boy went with his mother to dine at the parental residence of the sugar plantation empress; but while the grown people got along pleasantly and amicably together, the released captive, with liveliest recollections of his former imprisonment, kept a wide distance between himself and his former enslaver. If he could prevent it, he was determined that no such exercise of royalty should be visited upon him again; so the lad wandered about under the majestic shade trees and over the lawn, and feasted his eyes on the billowy ocean of cotton and cane that stretched for miles in every direction.

Several years after this came the Civil War; then the "Surrender," and the freeing of the slaves. These occurrences swept away much of the family fortune, but as Mr. A., the father of the empress, had great land possessions, he was still a very rich man.

Of course, the daughter, with her remarkable beauty and large wealth, did not lack for attention, and so she swept along her triumphant way looking and acting more like a royal personage than ever. Wherever she went she left a whole string of bleeding masculine hearts behind her, and all more or less broken in reality or imagination.

Soon after this came a piece of news about her that was so surprising that hundreds of tongues were set going for months. The tidings was that the heiress had become engaged to a prominent and unexceptionable young man of her own set, the marriage was celebrated in the stately old home mansion in the most elegant and sumptuous way, the guests departed at midnight, and the household retired. But the next morning the young and newly-wedded couple parted forever. They never ate a single meal together, and never saw or spoke to each other again. By mutual consent a divorce was speedily obtained. And today, after a lapse of thirty-eight years, the world is no wiser than it was then, as to the cause of the unhappy separation.

Both were persons who could keep a secret, and if the father and mother understood the cause of the trouble they never told anyone. The nearest friends and relatives were kept in ignorance of this strange, melancholy piece of family history. Of course there was much guessing and speculation, but conjecture is not certainty. The conviction, however, was general that the man was not at fault, but the trouble lay at the door of the haughty, hasty, imperious spirit of the empress.

Some years later the young man married again and has today, we are informed, a happy home and lovely family circle; but the empress never embarked in matrimony again.

Several years after this the parents died and left the young woman the lonely occupant of the great mansion where she had so long reigned and witnessed so many of her social triumphs. She became quite a recluse, and it would not be difficult to imagine the loneliness of her heart and the emptiness of her life.

One of her sorrows at this time came on the line of retribution. When people saw that she avoided them, they in turn left her to herself. The world has a way of striking back, and does not propose to grieve and break its heart over one of its absentees. When people take the notion to become hermits and draw away from others in a sulky mood, the rule is to let them go and have the spell out with themselves. This, of course, is provoking to the sulker, and especially to one who has had his or her own way for ever so long, but it is certainly good for the sulks itself. It also brings practical and very valuable lessons to the sulker.

The empress, however, remained a proud woman, and if the Spartan Fox was biting and eating, the cloak was wrapped around the gnawing and the gnawed spot, and no word was uttered.

Other sorrows still awaited the abdicated sovereign. The lawyers, in settling up the estate of Mr. A., found that the whole property was heavily mortgaged, and for far more than it could possibly bring for its sale. In better times something handsome might have been realized for the daughter, but the period of foreclosure was at a time of general financial depression, and so, after the business settlement, it was discovered that nothing of the great estate was left. The empress was without a throne, and stripped of an income. In a word, she was homeless and penniless.

She never asked relatives or friends for assistance. We doubt not if she had they would have helped her; but pride came in again and would not allow the humiliation. It is hard for one who has been a queen to become a dependent; for one who has sat on a throne to sit down as a second table kind of guest or hanger-on of some family. The young woman found something in her that made such a course impossible; so she went to a large city and took in sewing for a living.

But she was no skilled seamstress; she had owned servants who had performed all that kind of work for her, and the little she had done was not sufficient to make her anything like a swift and accomplished needlewoman. And so she could not make enough to properly support herself. Her comparatively inferior work caused her to lose patrons. Repeatedly she had to walk long distances to collect a single bill owed her by some wealthy woman, who did not dream of her former wealth and station. They were the empresses now, and she had to submit to their fault-finding, high words, and royal way of walking around and over ordinary folks.

She was finally compelled to move to a garret, cold, bleak, ill-furnished and generally miserable. Here she spent the last two years of her life in the vain attempt with her needle to keep body and soul together.

One day she was missed, and then another, and still another. On instituting a search they found her lying dead on her bed. Not a scrap of food, nor a single cent of money could be found in the room. The signs were that she had passed away in great agony.

On holding a post-mortem examination, the doctors announced that she had died of actual starvation!

When the friends and relatives in their distant homes and plantations heard of this dreadful end, they were profoundly shocked and distressed. But their grief did not alter facts. The empress had perished for lack of the common necessaries of life. She had slowly but surely starved to death.

Her friends and kindred bought a beautiful casket for the dead young woman, and had a silver plate put on the coffin lid, with the words, "At Rest." As to the truth of its application we can only hope; but concerning the appropriateness of another inscription, and one taken from the Bible, there cannot be the shadow of a doubt. The verse is found in Proverbs and reads as follows:

"Pride goeth before destruction, and a haughty spirit before a fall."

XV.

The Man in a Bog

In the swamps of Mississippi there are bayous and cypress brakes that are crossed by the traveler with difficulty in the best seasons of the year, and that in the rainy period of winter cannot be forded at all. To slip from the low bridge of logs laid over these sloughs means an immediate and hopeless miring down in the black, sticky mud. Even the wild denizens of the forest know better than to venture into one of these marshes to quench thirst; while domestic animals, like horses and cattle, if once entangled in such a quagmire, are doomed. For, while it is true that the "bog" has not the depth of the quicksand, yet it is deep enough and strong enough to hold the struggling creature fast, and bring all his frenzied efforts to escape to naught. With strength exhausted after many violent surgings and plungings, the victim seems to recognize its coming fate. So with a few additional feeble struggles, each one weaker than its predecessor, and now already half buried in the black ooze and slime, the unfortunate animal lies still, awaiting death, while buzzards perched upon surrounding trees tarry for the last breath before beginning their ghastly banquet.

Sometimes a human being gets into the toils of the marsh or bog, and finds it to be a grave. One instance out of a number comes up most vividly to the memory of the writer.

His aunt owned a plantation twelve miles from the county seat. To this place she was accustomed to send much of her cotton by means of ox wagons. On a cold winter day one of her teamsters drove an accustomed load to town in a wagon drawn by three yoke of oxen. After rolling the bales into a warehouse, the driver filled his vehicle with boxes and barrels of groceries, and started back late in the afternoon for the distant plantation. At nightfall he came to a place where he had the choice of mounting a long, steep hill, or taking a near cut through the swamp. The fact that the last mentioned road was nearer, was level and missed the lofty hill, decided the teamster, but he forgot how the constant autumn and winter rains had been at work on the turfy, sticky marsh, and had made it a quagmire almost impassable for any kind of vehicle, much less a heavily loaded wagon.

When he turned his team into this dark swamp road, this was the last seen of him in life. He did not arrive at home that night, nor at noon the next day, and so a party started out on horseback to search for him; and a little before dusk they came upon the following ghastly sight:

All of the oxen were mired down. Two were dead. The wagon was half tilted over, while the wheels on one side were so sunk in the bog that the hubs were out of sight. Several barrels and boxes were on the side of the road, a few fence rails scattered about where the driver had been trying to pry the wheels out of the deep ruts, and close by, lying flat on the mud, with his face upturned to the sky, was the negro stone dead!

He had gone to the farther side of the wagon, where the marsh was deepest, and there had stuck fast. From all the signs he had evidently made desperate efforts to get released, but, becoming weaker with every effort, found himself unable to pull his limbs out of the sticky death-trap, and so, in exhaustion and despair, fell backward and slowly froze to death. It required the strength of several men to draw the corpse from the bog, which seemed to hold the dead body with its black, entwining arms and reluctant to give it up.

There are worse bogs than those in the Yazoo Delta. There is something deadlier than a Mississippi marsh. There is a morass which not only destroys the body but damns the soul. It is called Sin! In it not simply individuals, but nations, are floundering, sinking, and perishing!

Men are caught in different sloughs and brakes of iniquity, but it is the same old sticky, blinding, choking, strangling, murdering bog of Sin. The rule is that he who goes out far, never gets back to the shore of safety. He sinks deeper with every oath, with every unclean thought, with every wrong word and act, and with every glass of liquor.

If it is the intemperance slough he is in, he flounders for a while, makes promises, swears off, joins societies, begins afresh on the New Year, and then on his birthday, but after all these endeavors at recovery, and in spite of all, he goes out farther, and settles down deeper in the bog than ever before. Men wave their hands to him and warn him, but all to no purpose. Their calls seem to be unheard and anyhow unheeded.

Meantime the efforts of the victim himself, to escape from his entanglements, become feebler, until finally every eye can see that all struggling has ceased. The man seems to realize that Sin has mastered him, and now lies down in its ooze and slime to die in silence and despair, while devils roosting around wait for the last breath, to pounce upon and fly off with the lost soul.

We once knew a young man who was a trusted bookkeeper in a large store. He was the support of a widowed sister and her three little girls. No father or husband could have been more thoughtful, kind and devoted. In addition to the comfortable home provided for them, he was considerate of their welfare and pleasure in many other ways too numerous to mention.

This young man, whose name was K., was exceedingly social in nature, with a leaning towards conviviality. Bright, witty, well read, and good-looking, he was greatly sought after for dinings, receptions and parties, and was indeed one of the first names among the gentlemen written down when lists of guests were being prepared. "We cannot get along without Mr. K.," was a speech uttered not only many times, but in many quarters.

In men's clubs and midnight suppers K. was in equal demand; and so it was that between the two he grew first familiar with the different wines and then fond of their taste and effect.

It was at this time we vividly recall him as popular with the various social circles in town, he was kept busy answering their invitations and meeting their demands. We saw him whirling along in carriages with ladies, and dashing past in buggies with gentlemen, and to all appearances absorbed and delighted with the life.

Again, we often beheld him on the street at an evening hour observed by the society element in the community as a time for public promenading. Whenever we saw him in these perambulations with young men and women, he would be talking earnestly, often laughing immoderately and affecting his companions with a like spirit.

We recall even at this length of time a growing redness in his face, and an increasing nervousness and abruptness of manner. He presented the appearance, as we now can see, of a man living in a state of highest tension. A certain glassy look of the eyes and tremulousness of the hands, were confirmatory signs of the dissipated life. Already the man was in the bog!

Several years passed away, and a marked change was observable in the family of Mrs. D., the sister of K. She had resumed the anxious, sorrowful look which had been banished for a while after the death of her husband by the devotion of her brother. She not only quit visiting, but avoided company altogether, while the signs of scant living and seedy clothing were unmistakable both in herself and the little girls. The house was still kept scrupulously neat and clean, but one could not walk through the dining-room and kitchen without feeling in a strange sort of way that both larder and store room were empty. The sideboard had nothing on it or in it, but a few chilly white dishes, while through the blue wire of the safe not a sign of bread or meat was visible.

It was also noticeable that K.'s dress was not as it formerly had been; but bore the appearance of long usage and of having been repeatedly mended and cleaned. The seams of his coat were glazed, his shoes showed patches, and the hat was dotted with grease spots. The truth was that K. was parting with nearly all his salary for the privilege of living in the bog!

It was most pathetic at this time to see how the man's sister and nieces would meet him when he came home from the store in the evening. The children were devoted to their uncle, but feeling the change in him, knew hardly how to act; while the sister clung to him, but in a way that has been described as "hoping against hope."

During this interval we never knew the man to laugh oftener and more immoderately. Especially was this true as he stood on the street corners with his companions, or was whirling past in a buggy with some chum. The instant he turned his face homeward a change would come over him, and while with those who loved him best and whom he was so cruelly wronging, he would be taciturn and moody. If spoken to, he would break forth in little nervous groans that were harder to hear and bear than his silence.

About this time a number of family circles dropped him, while others of a lower social grade took him up. While he said nothing, we doubt not that both occurrences sank like sharp arrows in his heart.

Soon after this he lost his position at the store. The merchant told him that he had for quite a while been making grave mistakes in his entries in the books, and in his accounts with customers, and he could not afford to employ him any longer. And so, from being chief bookkeeper at a salary of two hundred dollars a month, he was thrown out in the world without a penny.

The distress at the home was simply indescribable. The sister, Mrs. D., took in sewing, and the elder of the girls was taken from school and put out at service. The man who had been the support of the household now became the sponge of the family. His sister washed and ironed his linen, prepared his meals, slim enough as they were, and met him at the door at all hours of the night as, hiccoughing, grumbling, faultfinding and swearing, he would fumble around in the dark, unable to find the lock. She always met him kindly; and without a word of complaint or reproach would let him in and lead him to his bed, where he would sleep off his drunken stupor by the middle of the day.

All this time the man was getting deeper in the bog. Everybody could see it, while he apparently did not, but went on perfectly oblivious of his present shame, his increasing degradation and certain coming ruin.

With crimson face, disheveled hair and soiled and neglected dress, he was one of the most familiar objects on the street corners; and when not so drunk as to be in the gutter, as he often was, he would be laughing immoderately in a crowd of dissipated men like himself. We have seen him almost bent double while giving vent to these explosions of merriment, if the hollow, heart-sickening sound he made could be called by that name. But his laughter on these days was often of a solo character; for as men looked on the moral wreck before them, they had no heart to join in mirth over his jokes which, by the deadening effect of alcohol on the man's brain, had lost not only freshness and vigor but the point and meaning itself.

After this came several spells of delirium tremens. No maniac ever looked so terrible as did this man when the awful power of mania potu fell upon him. He raved, screamed, dashed the furniture to pieces, crouched in corners with pleading, staring eyes, and cried:

"They are after me! Take them off me! Mercy! Mercy! Mercy! Oh, horror! horror! horror!"

And then he would wallow and foam in agony on the floor.

The bog had the man!

After recovering from one of these spells, and looking like a corpse, and shaking like an aspen leaf, he would go right back upon another spree.

Some of his friends took him into the country and kept him for weeks amid the quiet, peaceful scenes of pastoral life. There, amid tinkling sheep bells, blooming orchards, cooing doves, whistling partridges and purling brooks they hoped to recall him to himself and to a better life. But the instant he returned to town he would rush to the drinking dens, beg, borrow or get money some way, and in a few hours would be picked up insensible out of the gutter.

Some who recall him at this time will never forget the emaciated figure, the zigzag movements of his body in walking, the sudden stops and startings off, the audible talking to himself, the spasmodic jerking of his head, with periodic pullings of his beard while attempting to look grave and wise, followed by a burst of senseless laughter on his part and a louder explosion of merriment from thoughtless boys on the street, who were watching and following him around. It is all so melancholy and dreadful that we pen these lines descriptive of an actual life history with the deepest pain.

The last attack of mania potu came after he had been drinking heavily for weeks. It required the strength of several men to keep him from leaping out of the window and otherwise killing himself. He thought his tongue was a dog, and tried to cut it with a knife. He cried out that "Snakes were in the room, and crawling toward him!" And with eyes dilated with horror and screaming "Help! Help! Help!" he would leap and dash himself here and there in the effort to escape from their imaginary presence until the perspiration streamed down his face and body, and he looked as if he would die from fright.

It was vain to speak to or lay the hand upon him. The slightest touch caused him to spring up in terror, while he did not seem to comprehend anything that was said to him. He was too far out in the bog! He only saw the sights and heard the sounds of the dreadful slough of Sin by which he had been entrapped and fastened, and into whose depths he was slowly disappearing from human view.

With snatches of ribald songs, scraps of jokes, partly uttered oaths, and a horrible laugh that as quickly died away into moans and whines, he passed through the last three hours of his life; when suddenly starting up from his bed he shrieked at the top of his voice so as to be heard all over the house and even on the street:

"Take them off me! Don't you see they are killing me! Murder! Murder! Murder!" And fell back upon his pillow in convulsions.

In ten minutes more he was dead.

The bog had done its work!

XVI.

A Lifetime Mistake

A lifetime mistake is one, as the words themselves indicate, which affects and pursues the chief actor up to the very door of his tomb. It is some mental or moral blunder which stamps its dark, sad impress of influence and consequence upon every year of the earthly life, escorts the individual up to the cemetery, and in many instances resumes the companionship on the other side of the grave. Of course there are sighs heaved, tears shed, and much suffering endured by the victim all along the weary months and years; but such things do not atone for the misdeed or mistake, and also fail as a deliverance from the peculiar affliction brought into the life by one's own hasty or deliberate choice or act.

The patient acceptance of the sorrow may bring about a weanedness from the world, and a corresponding development of the Christian character, but the peculiar trial remains. The fact that it was brought upon us by our own act adds to the bitterness of the life calamity.

Among these grave mistakes none seems to be more common than that of unwise marriages. The rushing mills of the divorce courts declare plainly in their own way how little thought and judgment were exercised by a great multitude of people in entering upon matrimony; while the unmistakable unhappiness and misery in countless households where the law is not resorted to for relief show as conclusively that the old adage is as true today as ever, where individuals are said to "marry in haste and repent at leisure."

The birds and animals, with all their inferiority, do not make the blunders of men and women when it comes to consorting; and even on their entrance into Noah's Ark, did so in pairs of a similar kind that indicated a certain level-headedness and wisdom which human beings might do well to imitate. What astonishment and laughter would have been occasioned if the lion had gone in with a cow, a tiger with a lamb, a goat with a monkey, and a giraffe with a rabbit!

But they did not, and we are compelled to look at the Human Race instead, to see the most absurd, incongruous and ill-assorted life companionships that the Fancy and Imagination could create in their wildest moments. The physical contrasts in the long with the short, and the fat with the lean is the smallest part of these marital infelicities. For graver even than Ugliness wedded to Beauty, we behold Refinement joined to Coarseness; Intellect to Ignorance; Character to Weakness; Goodness to Meanness; and Piety to Sin! Well might we say what on earth were people thinking of when they paid a preacher to join a portion of Heaven to a section of Hell, and then ask God in a concluding prayer to bless such a union.

In one of our large Southern cities lived a young man whom we shall call Alford. He was a member of the Methodist Church, had been clearly converted, was an active worker, and recognized by all as a spiritual man. He had been appointed steward and trustee, made a Sunday school teacher and finally promoted to the superintendency. Wherever he was placed he gave perfect satisfaction to the pastor and congregation.

The profession followed by Alford for a livelihood was that of the law. In it he had already distinguished himself as a fluent speaker, cogent reasoner and successful practitioner. He was conceded on all sides to be a steadily rising man, and making a fine income was evidently on his way to fortune as well as fame.

The Circuit Court in which he did much of his practice was composed of a number of towns in the State besides the city in which he lived. Twice a year he made flying trips to these various communities, according to his clients and briefs. In one of these localities, a mere village, he met his fate.

The destiny in this case was a young girl of seventeen or eighteen, with a pretty, doll-baby kind of a face, and a pair of penciled eyebrows, some flaxen hair on top of an empty skull, which in turn roofed over a shallow, hollow heart. The girl was good-looking but had neither sense nor religion.

This combination of course is quite unfortunate for a woman, and equally deplorable for the man who marries her; for in the course of time the physical loveliness is certain to depart, and then, if there is neither brains nor piety to fall back on, the absence at the same time of three such desirable things as come-liness, character and intellect makes a most startling and dis-tressing vacuity.

This is the reason that some men feel so completely undone and bankrupt in the home life. In their delusion they fancied they had captured all three of the above-named qualities, when they had simply married a French doll, or one of those highly dressed but most profoundly uninteresting figures we see posing in a milliner's or dressmaker's window. The infatuated man mistook pertness for intellect, and innocence, or, rather ignorance of the world, for character and spirituality. By and by, when the beauty of face departed, they looked for the other attributes, and lo! they were not, for they had never been!

At this interesting juncture men as a rule feel that they have been very badly treated, when the fact is that they are themselves to blame. They swallowed the bait without stopping to examine the hook and pole, and especially the individual on the bank who was angling for a husband.

Of course there is another side to all this, where a good woman has dropped her line in the stream and instead of catch-ing a fish landed an alligator, which proceeded to eat her up.

But in the case we are now considering all could see that the wrong and injury came from the woman to the man. The girl was nothing but a little social butterfly. And yet a gifted, sensible man married her! A lawyer who could unravel criminal myster-ies, and read character in the prisoner's dock and jury box at a glance, was completely taken in by a simpering, silly miss not out of her teens. He carried to his handsome home in the city, to be its queen and mistress, and to be his life-long companion and the mother of his children, something that under a faithful analysis resolved itself into a lawn dress with some pink ribbons, out of which peeped a small skull that was thatched with some fluffy blonde hair on the outside and furnished with almost next to nothing in the way of brains on the inside.

At first the man was amused with and interested in the frilled and furbelowed addition to his house; but in the course of a few weeks he had been rewarded with so many handfuls of empty air in return for clutches and grasps he had made upon his wife for something solid and substantial that a strangely anxious, troubled look began to gather in his eyes and settle in deep lines upon his face.

At her very entrance upon city life, this only child, petted and spoiled by her family, demanded to be taken everywhere to see the sights. She had been raised in a country town, had never beheld a great metropolis, and now wanted a general introduction to all its stars and lions, and immediate initiation into every one of its amusements.

The husband firmly remonstrated against going to the theater and opera, telling his wife that he was not only a member of the church but an official as well; that his attendance upon such places would not only be a violation of ecclesiastical law, but a reproach on Christianity.

Her reply was that he had been in the world and was surfeited; while she had never been anywhere nor seen anything that was worth talking about. She added that men were down town all day and saw much to interest, divert and please, while women had to be at home all the time, and knew nothing of what was going on in the world. As she had heard a number of her female friends say this she repeated it with great assurance, and with an appearance of being strikingly original. She wound up by saying that she just could not stand it to be cooped up that way; that it would have been better for her to have stayed at home with papa and mamma, and never married at all, etc., etc., etc.

This style of acting, kept up a few days, with the usual accompaniment of tears, coolness, and positive sulks, won the day at last; and so, starting out with concerts and socials, Alford, the young lawyer, was after a while beheld with his wife at the opera and theater, then on the ball-room floor, and finally at every kind of worldly entertainment.

The light soon left the man's face; he gave up his position as Sunday school superintendent, resigned from the Board of Stewards, became irregular in his attendance upon church, and at last ceased to come altogether.

Things went on this way for several years, when the writer of this sketch was appointed pastor of the charge where Alford and his wife held their membership. He saw with pain the unconverted state of the woman, and the backslidden condition of the man, but planned a protracted meeting and secured their promise to attend.

The lawyer broke his word and came only two or three times. The wife attended regularly, got under terrible conviction, and one night was brightly converted. Her husband happened to be present that evening, and we saw her with her face all aglow, rush to him, throw her arms about his form, and cry out, "Oh, Henry, I have got salvation! Come and get it, my husband! Don't you want it, Henry?"

Should we live to be a thousand years old we will never forget the cold, stony look he turned upon her. It was as though she had embraced the Sphinx! In the midst of all her joy she was staggered by the countenance he turned upon her. Her gladness changed into a whimper, and she placed her hand appealingly upon his shoulder; but the man never gave a sign that he recognized her presence or entreaty, while a dark, hard expression on the set face made it appear as if it was constructed out of iron.

Interpreted partially the look meant this, "Who are you to be talking to me in this manner? What right have you to speak to me about salvation, when it was your influence and life that led me from duty and from God!"

The silliness, shallowness and ignorance of the woman were to be seen even in this demonstrative rush upon her husband. Here she was expecting to undo in a moment an evil work which had cost her years to accomplish. She had stolen from the man his Christian faith, hope and joy, by a course of systematic opposition as well as temptation, and yet expected to restore it all in a moment with a wave of the hand and a chuck under the chin.

She had led her husband astray; could she not bring him back? Very likely this question arose in her mind, and we do not doubt that the same query has been asked by countless aching hearts before and since.

The answer is beheld all around us in hopelessly ruined lives!

It seems that we are powerless to recover those whom we personally led astray. There are exceptions, but the rule is the other way, as presented in this sketch. The fearful fact so constantly revealed in life is, that one can drag another from the light into darkness, and afterwards himself get back into light, but the one pulled down as a rule remains pulled down. Even when they are restored it will be, and must be, by another hand than that which drew them from God into sin. The reason for this must be evident to any spiritual thinker; while the fact itself brings to the breast of the repenting wrongdoer the keenest regret and suffering.

Alford and his wife are still living, although nearly twenty years have passed by since the scene described in the protracted meeting. The woman is what is called an active worker in the church, and has a little spiritual life; but she bears upon her face a settled melancholy that is evident to the most careless observer.

Alford became a prominent man, made money, but has evidently lost his soul. It is already lost according to the Bible. He is a ward politician, is immersed in the cares and business of this world, and living without hope and without God in the world. Foul-mouthed, profane, scented with tobacco and bloated with beer, it would be impossible to recognize in the hard-featured moral wreck the handsome, pure-faced, devoted young Christian whom a number of older citizens still remember, and recall with deepest sorrow of heart, because, in truth, he is no more.

Poor fellow! There are two passages of Scripture that we imagine he can never hear without a pang. One was spoken in the Garden of Eden when the blight and sorrow of sin had fallen, and God was locating the trouble. To the question, Why have you done this? the answer was reluctantly but truthfully given in the words: "The woman whom thou gavest to be with me."

The other passage is in the Gospel. It represents a principle as well as describes a fact. It reads thus:

"The hand that betrayeth me is with me on the table."

XVII.

The Face in the Ceiling

There are many strange things taking place all around us, that are as remarkable as any creation of Fancy or labored work of fiction. There are happenings at times in human lives which so encroach upon the supernatural as to defy all explanations of human reason. If narrated by persons of excitable and nervous temperament, we might obtain some light on the peculiar trans-actions, but told by persons of acknowledged level heads, steady nerves and unquestionable character, the matter reaches a point of mystery beyond all comprehension.

Once in a meeting led by the writer he had a morning audi-ence of fully one thousand people, while a half dozen preachers and laymen of the community sat in chairs upon the platform just behind the speaker.

At the conclusion of the sermon in one of these day serv-ices, we left the stand to talk and work with the seekers at the altar. As we did so a lady literally staggered toward us and, clutching our arm with a face as white as death, and turning a pair of horror-stricken eyes on one of the persons sitting on the platform, she fairly gasped:

"Oh, my God, Brother C., God has revealed yonder man to me! Oh, his face! It is all—all—oh, horror! horror!—" And the woman, trembling all over and unable to speak another word, covered her face and looked as if she would fall to the ground.

We said in reply, "My sister, what on earth is the matter with you?"

She lifted her face and, casting another look of consterna-tion, amazement and loathing upon a certain man on the plat-form, said:

"Must I tell you what I see? Must I tell you about his face?"

And again the expression of fear and disgust sprang up into her eyes and voice, while she looked like she would die with mental agony.

Seeing that her agitation was attracting attention, we replied:

"No. Say nothing and calm yourself. God can manage the man who so troubles you."

She obeyed tremblingly, but since then we have wondered whether we did right in checking her. As Peter exposed one character and Paul another enemy of the Gospel, how do we know but that the Spirit of God intended confusion, conviction and salvation from the incident?

All this is but an introduction to a curious circumstance which took place five or six years ago in one of the Southern States. The main party concerned was a minister of the Gospel in the Presbyterian Church. For years he had been an active, zealous servant of God, when the great temptation of his life arose, began its assault, siege and sapping work.

While no criminality stained his soul, yet an infatuation had set in, drawing his thoughts and affections in forbidden directions, until a frightful moral peril, increasing daily in danger, threatened his character and salvation.

The mutual weakness of the two began to be observed, and some, with watch and almanac in hand, placed themselves, so to speak, to note the expected crash and downfall.

At this critical time the preacher, now almost vanquished, retired one night to his room. He was sitting in a chair near a center table, upon which rested a lighted lamp, when, happening to look toward the fireplace, he beheld to his unutterable horror, an agonized human face just over the mantel and thrust partly out from the wall! It was the countenance of the man whom he was on the verge of wronging in the darkest and most dishonorable manner. The face was convulsed; the eyes were turned upon him with such fury and hate that they looked as if they would burst from the head; the veins were swollen and the whole appearance that of a man longing to murder the being upon whom he was gazing.

The spectacle was so horrifying to the guilty conscience that the convicted man drew a large knife from his pocket and drove the blade into his breast just over the heart. As he did so he fell upon the floor, face uppermost, with the blood gushing from the wound, while the knife handle quivered and shook with the beating of the heart just beneath.

Momentarily expecting death, the unhappy preacher was afraid to look toward the mantel lest he should see again the dreadful apparition there, but, in a kind of mingled despair and supplication, cast his eyes upward, and to his amazement beheld a face, holy, pitiful and yet aggrieved, looking down upon him from the ceiling.

The lamp from the table threw a ring of light on the wall above, and right in this circle, which seemed like a halo, appeared this loving, melancholy, rebuking countenance. There was a peculiar glory resting upon it, and he felt in his inmost soul that it was Christ who was casting upon him that sorrowful, reproachful gaze. The face, while showing compassion, yet had also a commanding, protesting expression. Translated into language it would have read, "Do thyself no harm."

At this moment the wounded man lost consciousness, and the next morning was found by the members of the household lying on the floor and weltering in blood which trickled slowly from the wound, while the knife thrust up to the haft in the breast was still giving that quivering, oscillating movement in answer to the throb of the miserable heart close by.

The stab was not a fatal one, and in the course of a few days the subject of this sketch was out again, but bearing a deeper wound on his soul than the blade had given his body.

Up to this time he had been a great ridiculer and opposer of holiness, insisting that no man could live without sin in this world. But there was something in the two faces that looked upon him that night which made him wish to leave all sin forever. He conceived an unutterable horror of going to a world where agonized spirits glare on each other, and came into as great a longing for a country where the King's face, in its love, purity and truth, is the light and glory of the land. The fight against sanctification and sanctified people was all taken out of him, and he became the most thoughtful and melancholy of men.

At this time the papers announced the holding of a holiness convention in a large city not far from where the preacher lived. Without declaring his intention to anyone, he made his arrangements to attend, determining, if there was truth in the doctrine and experience, he would find it out, and get rid of a "body of sin and death" which seemed to be located in his spirit somewhere, and that kept him bowed down as with a load almost continually. He had before this received pardon for his sins of thought and desire and for his attempted suicide. It was not forgiveness he wanted now, but deliverance, freedom, purity, holiness!

So he came to the city, arriving on the third night of the meeting. As he took his seat in the Tabernacle, he heard the people speaking in whispers around him of the power that had already come down. He found arising in him a strange interest in and desire to see the evangelist who was conducting the services.

The building began to fill up rapidly, while the hands of the clock were approaching the minute when worship would begin. Preachers and laymen came in and took seats upon the platform, while whispering people would say, "There he is," "No, that is not the man," etc., etc.

At last, just as the hands pointed to half-past seven, a man walked upon the platform from a side door, and knelt for several minutes by a chair, with his head bowed low. For some reason the visiting preacher felt his eyes riveted on the kneeling figure. He could not account for it, but his interest was almost a breathless one in a person whose face he had not yet seen. He felt without being told that the man praying was the evangelist, and there was a strange thrill upon him that this man was to affect his life in some powerful way.

Suddenly the evangelist arose and took his seat with his face toward the congregation and fronting in a straight line with the visitor. To the preacher's unspeakable amazement he saw shining on the countenance of the evangelist the same peculiar light and glory he had beheld on the face which had gazed upon him from the ceiling!

His emotion was so great that he could scarcely control himself, and but for the opening volume of song would have doubtless cried out. Little by little, however, the strange fact translated itself to his mind after this manner:

"God is in all this. There is His servant and he will bring me a message. The light and strange glory I see upon him is the Lord's endorsement and introduction of His messenger, and is a bidding to me to listen, believe and receive. By the grace of God I will."

And he did. As the sermon proceeded and the truth was unfolded, he saw the human need and the divine supply, the plague and the remedy of sin. He saw the possibility of obtaining a pure heart filled with perfect love, not as a development, but as an instantaneous work of grace wrought in the consecrated and believing soul.

At the conclusion of the sermon, he came all broken to the altar, and went again and again, until, on the fourth night of his public seeking, he found the pearl of great price, full salvation from all sin.

This was six years ago; and it was only last summer that we met him and had his story from his own lips. And, judging from the light in his face, the gladness in his eyes and voice, and the unmistakable peace in his soul, he was undergoing no regret whatever, that he had sought with all his heart, and given up all that he was and possessed, and had received in exchange the blessing of a restful, holy heart.

XVIII.

A Long-time Sufferer

Two remarkable things about human life are bound to impress the observer in the course of a very short time. One is the compensating feature of the divine providence. That is when people are seen to be maimed, afflicted or poverty stricken, a second study of the case reveals them in the possession of some new talent, gift, beauty of person or possession of wealth which shows that if for some reasons they are to be pitied, there are still other circumstances in the case that call for admiration and congratulation. The invalid is discovered to be an author or gifted musician. The hunchback has a fortune, etc., etc.

On the other hand, in the study of the great human procession before us, we find what might be called the drawbacks and discounts of life. That is, we find people of fortune, station, wisdom, wit, beauty and fame fairly borne down and crushed with some kind of malady, affliction, sorrow, trial or physical suffering that dashes with bitterness the whole cup of life.

Miss Edgeworth, in one of her works, tells of a woman of fashion and an envied ruler in high circles who would have to retire from her receptions into a private room to hide the paroxysms of pain occasioned by a cancer on the breast. One of our leading generals, famous around the world, suffered excruciating anguish for years and finally died from the effects of a fearful disease of the tongue and throat. Two of the reigning monarchs of Europe today are martyrs to physical pain that amounts to torture.

The Bible recognizes this state of things without comment, in the quiet statement that Naaman, the captain of the hosts of the King of Syria, was a great man with his master, but he was a leper!

A New-Yorker, standing on Fifth avenue one night, pointed out to a friend a number of elegant brown-stone mansions, and stated in connection with each one some ghastly, grizzly, sorrowful fact of family history that was bound to make the inmates of those palaces heave as heavy sighs and weep as bitter tears as are heard and seen in the abodes of poverty in the slums of the same city. There seems to be some kind of presiding justice, some equalizing agency in life, which divides out blessings and afflictions in the human race, preventing prosperity from running mad in this place, and adversity from sinking in despair over yonder. So a weight is needed for one man, and a wing must be attached to another, and an anchor fastened to still another.

Sometimes the life seems to be all gaiety; but we have only to wait to see that the burdens finally come, and those happenings to heart, mind, soul and body take place which give the grave, thoughtful lines to the face, the increasing slowness to speak, the growing pity and charity to men, the weanedness from this earth, and, in a word, that better condition for entrance upon a world and life where destiny is fixed, character and goodness constitute the rank, and the King is Immutable! Omnipotent! Eternal! and above all, Holy!

In one of our Southern towns dwelt a woman who was the occasion of envy to many hundreds of hearts. She was beautiful, to begin with, was educated and accomplished, possessed wealth, moved in what is called the best social circles, married well, had a lovely family of three sons and a daughter, and owned one of the handsomest homes in the town where she lived.

This lady was a Methodist, but scarcely ever attended church. The temple of worship was only two blocks from the house, and its great bell summoning its congregation could be heard even through the thick walls and closed doors of the family mansion. She in after years confessed that the sound disturbed her. She said it had an accent of invitation and entreaty, and seemed to say, with its solemn swing and deep-toned note, "Come! Come! Come!"

But why go? According to earthly light and wisdom she did not need to go. Did she not possess everything dear to a woman's heart? Were not her husband and children devoted to her? Were they not all well? Did she not have friends and money in abundance? What need to go? Churches doubtless were very good for the disappointed, afflicted and heartbroken of earth, but she had suffered no bereavement, lost no fortune or friends; what need, then, for her to attend? Her household circle was unbroken, and she had never known what it was to have a serious spell of sickness. No, the bell might ring on, but she was not going! She had all she wanted right around her.

It would be impossible to tell how many people who passed down that street, and, glancing over the lawn and flower yard at the stately dwelling, surrounded by large shade trees, felt that they would gladly exchange places with such an obviously blessed and favored woman.

It would not require much spiritual wisdom for a person to see that the things in this life which absorb our attention, engross our affection and take up our time are the rivals of God and the enemies of our soul. In the faithful dealing and providence of the Almighty, false deities are struck at and idols have to go. Men would be spared more suffering in this world if they did not bow down in false worship and make divinities of flesh, mud and metal.

In the fullness of time the clouds gathered, the winds arose, and the cyclone fell. The husband, a son and daughter died; a second boy wandered from home and was heard of no more, and the third became a drunkard. Then the fortune took wings and vanished, the home went under the auctioneer's hammer, and the sorrowing woman took refuge in an humble cottage nearby. For years her health had been going down, and now she became a hopeless invalid.

Her disease was a peculiar form of rheumatism, which horribly misshaped her limbs, drew her wrists awry, and twisted her fingers until they looked uncanny and not human like. For the first few years she was able to do a little crochet work, but as the cramping and bending of the hands went on, even this simple task became impossible, and, all curved in body and with two bunches of fingers held before her, all pointing in different directions, she sat in an invalid chair day after day, month after month, and year after year with nothing to do but to think and suffer, and suffer and think.

When we first saw her, through the request of her pastor, she had been in this condition seventeen years. She had been such a sufferer that all of her splendid beauty was gone; while the shock we realized on beholding the doubled-up form and the glazed-looking, talon-like fingers is remembered powerfully to this day.

The deeply afflicted woman lived seven years after that before Death relieved her from her sufferings. She told the writer, on the visit just mentioned, that she never knew a single instant when she was free from pain. To this martyrdom of seventeen years was added, as we have said, seven more, so that she was in the furnace of physical affliction a quarter of a century lacking just twelve months.

It is with deep gratification we record the fact that when the great troubles of the woman's life came rolling in upon her like the billows of an ocean, she turned to God. Instead of engulfing, these waves under the blessing of heaven, tossed her soul to the feet of Christ. Widowed, childless, beggared, homeless, lonely, wrecked in health and all but friendless, she called on God, was heard in that she feared, and was delivered and carried from that time like a lamb in the bosom of the divine Shepherd.

At the time we first beheld her she had been a saint for years. The invalid chair had become a throne, she was the recognized daughter of the King of Heaven, a princess of Royal birth, and exercised a holy rulership which all felt the instant they entered her presence.

From the wreck of the physical comeliness came up a moral and spiritual loveliness which simply defied description. It was the beauty of holiness. It was a benediction to the eye and soul to look upon her restful, shining countenance.

From the hour she obtained Full Salvation, she never was heard to murmur or utter a complaint of any kind. Even when she said she was never without pain she spoke so sweetly and quietly that one could scarcely realize the truth of her statement, until it was confirmed by her physician.

People from all over town came to her for advice, sympathy and comfort in trouble. She never failed to give what was needed, and hundreds went away from the throne-room of this princess of grace renewed, refilled, refired and in some way better prepared for the sufferings, toils and battles of life. They came to the physically weak and she, all powerful through the Lord whom she loved and served, helped them to spiritual life and strength.

The writer had been asked to call on her and pray with her; but as we entered the room and looked upon her face, we saw that, in spite of the bent and emaciated body, one of Heaven's Queens was before us. Instead of praying for her, we felt strongly inclined to bow down at once and beg her to pray for us. We went there to do her good, but God is our witness that she blessed us far more than we helped her.

After a long and victorious reign of twenty years, subsequent to her becoming a spiritual queen and ascending the throne, she left the invalid chair, got into a chariot of fire, and went up to her Father's Heavenly Kingdom. The poor afflicted body was so twisted and bent that it could not be placed in a coffin, so they boxed up with plank the wooden seat, with its silent, pulseless occupant, and buried her thus in the cemetery.

There the body is today sitting upright and waiting for the coming and voice of the Son of God, who will summon her to arise and appear in resurrection glory and perfection, to suffer and die no more forever. The spirit of the released martyr has been in heaven now fully twenty years. We doubt not that face to face she has long ago thanked the King who saw fit to slay the body in order to save the soul, who changed her invalid chair to a throne, and who made her afflictions work out for her a far more exceeding and eternal weight of glory.

XIX.

The Bulger Family

The household circle that bore the name of Bulger consisted of the father, mother and five sons. As a rule they had but little to do with their neighbors, were counted unsocial, and seemed glad to be let alone.

Left to and centered in themselves one might have supposed that books, music and bright conversation would explain their independent attitude, and account for the flight of the hours which were spent in each other's presence. But the Bulger family had no literary tastes, hardly read anything, owned no musical instruments and spoke but rarely and briefly to one another.

All had stolid looking faces, and would sit for half an hour at a time around the fireside without saying a word while twirling their thumbs and solemnly batting their eyes. They also had a strange way of gazing fixedly at people, as if they were looking upon vacancy. It seemed as if they were trying to bore into and read the very inmost heart of the party before them, when in reality they were doing nothing of the kind. It was just a cow-like gaze they possessed.

Until one knew the family and its idiosyncrasies better it was quite uncomfortable to feel seven pairs of eyes all turned solemnly on the visitor, while the twirling thumbs seemed to be turning the victim over and over in exhaustive investigation, and the eyelids batted out the few moments left him to live in the world. Sometimes we have seen this household Inquisition keep up its oppressive silence, eye-batting and thumb-twisting for a full hour; the only change being some slight alteration of position in crossing, uncrossing or recrossing the limbs.

In the beginning of the acquaintance with the Bulgers, one was impressed with the necessity of breaking into this dreadful stillness and eye inquiry by some kind of remark. One felt like protesting and proving in some way that he was not as bad as the Bulgers seemed to think. Or humanity itself demanded that the Bulger mind should be relieved and diverted by the utterance of something pleasant, edifying, or even humorous. But it was all alike lost on the Bulgers. They either would or could not be entertained; so that every verbal sally was met with the batting eyelid, and literally rolled out of sight by the twirling thumbs.

On some of these occasions one of the family had been known to give a little grunt; or the corner of the mouth would twitch a moment; but as if to make up for such unbending, an increased gravity would settle in the manner and a deeper stolidity than ever appear in the face; so that the unfortunate speaker would be quite confused and overcome not to say frozen by this sudden running up against and discovery of the North Pole.

The old father was the most restless of the seven, if such a charge could be made of any of them. Once in awhile he would heave a sigh, turn in his seat, throw his arm over the back of his chair and gaze through his spectacles out of the window, and bat and blink as solemnly and wisely as though he was seated on the highest judicial bench, and settling the merits of the profoundest legal case in the country. So it seemed, for really his mind at times was as blank as his eyes looked. Some said he was really gazing at something, but that it was an inner history; and this contemplation brought the sigh, and the restless movement in the chair.

The mother in earlier years had been disposed to be talkative, and break up in a measure the family silence. But six household Gibraltars pounded her wavelets of attempted conversation to pieces, and so she had subsided into a corner, where she would knit for hours without a word, only stealing an occasional glance at her husband and sons. There was, however, this difference between them; she thought, while the others just looked like they were thinking; they simply batted!

The oldest son was the first to die, and almost immediately a whisper crept around about a couple of dark deeds attributable to him. This caused a more systematic shunning of the Bulgers, but they closed up ranks without a word and went on as soldiers do when comrades fall in battle.

In the course of a few years every son save Horace, the youngest, was in the cemetery, and it was curious that with each succeeding death a new whisper would arise and float about relative to some dark and criminal deed that had been committed by the dead man. So there were rumors of a deserted wife, a forged note and other unenviable transactions. If the Bulgers heard these reports they gave no sign, but simply closed up ranks each time, and stared with increasing stolidity at the fire.

They were reduced to three in number when suddenly the old man took to his bed, gathered up his feet, turned his face to the wall, stared it out of countenance, batted his eyes a number of times without saying a word, and was gone.

At this time the youngest and now only surviving son came to the front. He obtained a fine position in a large store and by steady devotion to business got to be looked on as one of the best young men of the town. He had the same peculiar grave countenance and silent manners of his departed father and brothers, but unlike them he seemed to be energetic and industrious and so won a certain public regard. In addition to his business punctuality he was courteous in his quiet way to all, careful in his dress, and never seen in a theatre, circus, billiard room or saloon.

After his mother left him to live with a favorite niece in a distant town, Horace Bulger rented a room over the store where he clerked, and when business hours were over could almost invariably be found in this apartment.

So his stock steadily rose in value in the social and commercial world, as both classes of people counted him a model young man, in every respect.

Several years passed and Horace became identified with one of the churches, was made an official member, and also elected librarian of the Sunday school. It was charming to see him in his black suit and immaculate linen, the pink of propriety, a model of gravity, while his books were as well kept as his Sabbath garments. He formed the text of many a mother's sermon or exhortation to her wandering boys, "Why don't you do like Horace Bulger?" "If I could see you sober and steady like Horace Bulger I could die in peace," etc., etc.

Perhaps of all classes of people, young Bulger was least popular with the wild boys and youths in town because they had been so often tongue-thrashed over the shoulders of his consistent and moral life.

One day a young man of another church was in the store being waited on by Horace. As the clerk was bundling up an article for his customer, he remarked in regard to some occurrence:

"That is as hard to believe as that I am a drinking man."

To this the purchaser said nothing, whereupon Bulger again asserted: "That is as hard to credit as a report would be that I am a drinking man."

And still there was a painful silence.

Bulger seemed strangely annoyed at the failure of the young man to make any response, and repeated the third time the same speech, and ended it with the question:

"Don't you think so?"

And the quiet but firm-faced man before him replied:

"If you insist on my speaking the truth, I would say that I think you are the hardest drinker in the city!"

The effect of this blunt and honest speech on Bulger was amazing. He turned as pale as death, and said with a choking voice:

"What have you seen in me that makes you think so?"

And the customer replied: "For months I have observed the unmistakable signs."

Bulger breathed heavily as he leaned against the counter and asked:

"Do you think anyone else has noticed it?"

"I believe," returned his rebuker, with a sorrowful and solemn face, "that your employer begins to suspect you."

The next moment the guilty man "went to pieces" as they say in criminal court language, and made the ghastly confession to the man standing before him that there was not a night that he did not empty four to six bottles of strong liquor, and was always under alcoholic influence in the day.

Pursuing his confession he said, in great agitation:

"I cannot help myself. My brothers were all secret drinkers, and so was my father before us. He himself inherited the same appetite from his father; so it came to my brothers and myself with a double power. It has got me! I am in chains, and can't break away, and don't want to. I was in hopes that I could drink in secret, keep up in public and attend to my work. But I see I cannot. I feel now that I am a doomed man!"

The friend before him offered counsel, encouragement and hope through Christ, but his words evidently fell on a dull and dead ear.

Bulger was never the same person after this. He became reckless and allowed his true character to be seen by the public. In less than three years he drank himself into a drunkard's grave.

His body lies in the cemetery in the same row with his father and four brothers, who in spite of their persistent silence became well known to men.

Evidently there must be another speech or language than that of the tongue by which we declare ourselves, and get to be accurately measured and properly branded at the hands of our fellow men.

*   *   *   *   *   *

Not long after these occurrences two gentlemen were conversing about the strangeness of the circumstance, when one said to the other:

"Do you know the lesson we learn from the ostrich?"

"I suppose that little heads and big plumes go together."

"No, sir; try again."

"Well, then, the smallest of heads may go with the largest of bodies."

"No. Your answers are good; but you have not given the right one yet."

"Then I give up."

"I am surprised at that, for the lesson I refer to is the one that should be the first to suggest itself. I mean the curious habit of the bird when pursued, of thrusting its little silly head in the sand and thinking its huge body is hidden. Here was Horace Bulger a confirmed drunkard and positively comfortable with the thought that not a soul knew it. He forgot that a man's actual life is bigger than what he says, and that character is as evident as outward conduct. He also failed to recognize that a small town is the shallowest of sand in which to hide the real man."

There was a few moments of silence when the speaker added:

"There are many who are trying to do the same thing today. They walk, write, gesticulate and vociferate one thing and are really another. Meantime they are under the marvelous delusion that everybody is as ignorant concerning their true selves, when the fact is that the big body of the real man is perfectly apparent to the thoughtful, while it is only the shallow head of the would-be deceiver that is under the sand."

There followed a moment of reflection, and the party addressed remarked, with a sigh:

"The ostrich family is a large one!"

"Yes," replied the other, "and quite a number of its members have moved from Africa to America."

XX.

A Human Cyclone

The famous Fourth of July was being celebrated in a southern town after the usual order of disorder, made up of shouting and yelling, brass-band playing, soldier parading, speechifying, firecrackers by day and skyrockets by night, with cannon-shooting at all hours.

Among the patriotic and tireless young men who managed the ten-pounder on a neighboring bluff, waking up the echoes in the surrounding hills and across the river, was a recent comer to the town who bore the name of Charley Hurrekan.

If ever there was truth and appropriateness in names our friend Charley possessed the right one in Hurrekan. It is true that phonetics rather than orthography brought up the association to the mind in this case, but it was not the less powerfully done, and no one could be with the man a couple of minutes, and then hear his name, without a smile springing to the lip which had its origin in a lively sense of the fitness of certain things, but concerning which fitness no one cared to speak with Mr. Hurrekan.

One striking fact connected with the breezy, stormy Mr. Hurrekan was his possession of a marvelous physical strength. His feats of lifting, hurling, boxing and wrestling had brought him into immediate notice and great fame with those who admire those kind of performances. No one cared to feel the force of his ironlike fist, but many considered it a high honor to have been allowed to touch the great swelling muscles of his herculean arm.

Another notable feature of the man was the fire that fairly gleamed and glittered in his black eyes when he turned them in anger on one; it gave a kind of shock, and as a painful experience ranked next to encountering his sledge-like fist.

It had fallen to the lot of our friend Charley on the celebration of the "Fourth" to sponge the cannon and ram in the load after each discharge; and he was doing this in his usual rapid, careless style when the gun went off of its own accord through the heated metal, and the young man lost his left arm and eye.

He was placed quickly in a litter and borne to an adjacent hotel, where physicians labored to save him, but with little hope. Later in the night a preacher, the presiding elder of the district, was called in to pray with the desperately wounded man. On what was supposed to be his deathbed, young Hurrekan professed faith in Christ, and was converted.

Being blessed with a wonderful constitution, the sick man did not die but lived; and in the days of his convalescence he told the minister who had visited him daily, that he wanted to enter into the active work of the ministry. But our convert's zeal cooled off when he recovered his health and he began to avoid the preacher who had been such a faithful friend. Nor was he sorry that the district duties of the elder called him away much of the time, preventing the looking up of the wanderer and his restoration to the fold.

Meantime the gigantic strength of the man returned, and it was said that the power of both members had gone into the right arm. He secured a false eye, and, appearing on the street, looked exactly like his former self but for the empty coat sleeve swinging by his left side.

A few months rolled by, when K—, the minister referred to above, was crossing the Mississippi River in a large ferry boat, and saw Hurrekan sitting in a fine two-horse rig driven by a negro in livery, while blazing sentences on the leather curtains of the vehicle declared the manifold virtues of some kind of patent medicine. K— looked gravely at the head and chief of this rainbow affair, and Hurrekan winced and directed his gaze down the river.

At the Terminal Depot, the newly-fledged doctor turned his horses and wagon over to the railroad agent to be shipped to him on the next freight, and then hurried away to catch the passenger train. He and his gaily-dressed servant entered one of the coaches, and after a little began unpacking a nice-looking basket, displaying thereby a luncheon of broiled chicken, beef tongue, pickles, a salad and light bread. Last he drew forth a bottle of wine and glass tumbler.

Just then, happening to glance up, he saw K— only a few feet away silently contemplating him. The eyes of Hurrekan instantly fell to the floor, and a deep red stole into his face. There was also an immediate loss of appetite, and the tempting food was soon given to the ebony attendant sitting just behind him. After he did this, the worried man turned his body slightly and fastened a dejected look through the window on the flying scenery outside.

In another moment K— took the vacant seat by his side and, laying his hand on Hurrekan's shoulder, said:

"Do you think that you are treating the Lord right?"

"No, I don't," the Jonah answered, striking the bench before him a heavy blow with his big fist.

"What are you going to do about it?" persisted K—.

In reply Hurrekan leaned forward and, taking first the bottle and then the glass in his hand, threw them one after another through the open window. Then turning to K—, with a resolute look, he said:

"I'm going to do the clean and right thing."

"I rejoice to hear you say so," replied K—. "Do I understand you to be willing to go forth and work for Christ on a poor circuit for slim wages?"

"Yes, if He will forgive me for my past failure and faithlessness." And tears sprang into the man's eyes.

"He will do it," returned K—.

"He has already done it," cried Hurrekan, looking up with a beaming face.

The hands of the two men met, and propositions were made and plans agreed upon.

The result was that Hurrekan promised K— to meet him at his next quarterly conference a week later. He left the train at the first large town, where he sold his gaudy wagon and richly caparisoned horses, paid off and discharged his servant, and then, according to promise, overtook K— in a town fifty miles away.

Here he joined the church one day, and was licensed to exercise his gifts as a local preacher on the next. K— then sent him nearly one hundred miles off as a supply to a circuit which had lost its regular pastor. He said in parting with his late acquisition:

"I turn you loose on that country. They need just such a man as yourself."

Now, in "turning Hurrekan loose" was indeed the loosing of a hurricane; and so the people of that faraway circuit found out with a vengeance. On being asked after the first round how they liked their new preacher, they looked bewildered and strikingly like men who had just passed through a cyclone.

The first thing that the Rev. Mr. Hurrekan did after devoting several days to the study of his flock and receiving reports about them, was to throw the church register into the fire with the simple and startling explanation:

"Not one of you are fit to be in the church, and I am going to make every one of you join over again and start afresh."

And they did; for the pounding of that great fist on the sacred desk, and the blazing of that right eye in the pulpit seemed to leave no other course open for them.

One day in one of his meetings a couple of young men made a disturbance in the congregation, whereupon Hurrekan closed the Bible from which he was reading, walked down the aisle and deliberately collaring one of them, lifted him bodily from his seat, trotted the amazed man to the door and pitched him into the yard. Returning to the second offender who sat almost paralyzed in the pew, he served him after an identical fashion.

Of course, all this packed the new preacher's church, and at the same time secured the very best attention, and a most respectful hearing. Another thing which contributed to the good order was, that Hurrekan could not close his eyelid over the glass eye which he wore; and no one knowing that he had but one organ of sight supposed that he was praying with one eye open in order to catch some transgressor. So the sight of that big black optic staring fixedly on the audience, and backed up as it was with that sledge-hammer fist, inspired a stillness in the congregation and a decorum that for perfectness had never been known before in those regions.

In the summer our hero attended a camp meeting, where the order was anything but good. Coming into the service late one day, Hurrekan sat in the rear of the tabernacle and several seats in front of three young men who were acting outrageously. He turned several times and told them to behave themselves, but they rather grew worse, when suddenly he fixed his blazing eye upon the group and started for them. Perfectly panic-struck and not waiting to reach the aisle they tumbled over the benches, and over one another in their frantic efforts to escape. Hurrekan was so close upon them, however, that there was nothing left them but to make a flying leap over a barbed wire fence which surrounded the grounds. This they just managed to do, but not without leaving small portions of their garments on the little spearheads where they fluttered for several days to the great amusement of many who had them pointed out while being told the story.

Just before Conference, K— held his fourth quarterly meeting in a town on Hurrekan's circuit, where that clerical gentleman was least known. On Saturday the two preachers were eating dinner together at the hotel and quietly talking about the prospects of the pastoral charge. At another table sat a group of men who were evidently drinking and disposed to be noisy. One in especial conceived, as he thought, a brilliant plan of having a great deal of fun out of two preachers, one of whom had only one arm, while the other was a grave, quiet sort of individual.

So, taking up a bottle of liquor from his table, and pretending to be more intoxicated than he was, the man walked over to the ministers and declared that he wanted them to drink with him, and started to pour the red liquid in their glasses.

Hurrekan looked up at the man with a dangerous gleam in his eye and said:

"We do not drink, sir."

"But I want you to drink," was his reply, "and what is more I am determined that you shall."

Hurrekan, in a voice of suppressed passion and with lightning in his eye, said:

"My friend, if you were aware of it, you are at present in an exceedingly unhealthy place for yourself."

The only notice that the obtruder took of this speech was to endeavor with an unsteady hand to fill the preacher's glass with whisky, when, quick as an electric flash from the skies, Hurrekan was on his feet, and with that marvelous right hand and arm had caught the astounded person by the throat, lifted him entirely from the floor and shot him through the air for a distance of ten feet and landed him with a crash amid the chairs. Before the man could arise Hurrekan was upon him again, jerked him up and pinioned him against the wall with his long powerful fingers about his neck.

While he held his prisoner in this garroting style, the preacher proceeded to address some caustic remarks to the choking and badly frightened man. Among other things, he enlarged upon the wisdom of being polite to strangers; and the exceeding advisability of letting people alone with whom he had no business; and if he would do such things, then the good sense in finding out their strength before attacking them.

With this lecture, as Hurrekan called it, and for which he told the man he charged him nothing, he suddenly shifted his hand, caught him by the back of his neck and propelled him at a two-forty pace through the room, out on the gallery and fired him like a catapult down the front steps into the street. The man, now thoroughly terrorized and also sobered, struck the ground running and kept up the gait the preacher had initiated him into, and as far as he could be seen was making tracks for some unknown refuge or asylum of rest.

At the Annual Conference in December, K—, Hurrekan, and the writer were assigned to the home of a sweet-faced elderly lady who was a member of the Methodist Church.

As we listened to the loud tones and marked the stormy ways of our demonstrative friend in this quiet family, we were in actual pain for him and our entertainer. But to our surprise the lady showed not the least sign of displeasure, but the contrary.

One morning in our bedroom, something was said of a humorous nature which so tickled our hero that he burst into shouts of laughter and stentorian yells, while striking his fist on a little center table with great hammer-like blows which threatened to crush that piece of furniture, made everything on the mantel jingle and jump, and shook even the house.

We went out to breakfast feeling deeply mortified over the affair and especially sorry for Hurrekan. So we fully expected to see an offended look on the face of our hostess; but to our amazement her countenance fairly beamed on our Boanerges, and she had him to sit next to her, and kept his plate heaped with the best on the table.

Several mornings after this, we three were walking through the back yard, when Hurrekan, spying a small sharp-roofed coop about four feet high with a big turkey gobbler in it, fattening for the table, immediately cried out to us:

"Watch me jump the thing!"

And running towards the little structure he attempted to clear it, when seeing he could not, he kicked it over as he arose in the air; whereupon the turkey got out with a tremendous amount of gobblings and flutterings, and then a perfect pandemonium reigned for several minutes in the yard made up of barking dogs, squalling chickens, sputtering cats and laughing negroes, until the din and uproar were terrific.

Feeling genuinely distressed and chagrined for Hurrekan, who was hallooing at the top of his voice, we glanced anxiously at the house and there beheld our hostess standing on the back gallery with her face wreathed in smiles and surveying the noisy scene and the author of it with the highest good humor and approval.

To crown all, on the last day of the Conference when we were leaving the hospitable home and bidding our kind entertainer adieu, she gave K— and the writer a friendly clasp of the hand, but in Hurrekan's palm she slipped a twenty-dollar bill!

After this we lost sight of our obstreperous friend for several years. Having been sent to a distant city, not so much as a rumor reached us concerning him.

One day, while on a return trip, we saw him standing in front of a store, the meekest and quietest looking of men. We spoke to him, expecting the old-time loud laugh and stormy outburst; but nothing of the kind happened. We were in his presence an hour and failed to witness the least particle of the former boisterousness and noisiness. We of course could not with any propriety ask him what was the matter, but we were amazed all the same and left him with a deep wonder relative to the silent, meek, and subdued-looking man.

The next day we met a mutual friend and said at once:

"What on earth is the matter with Hurrekan? We never saw a man as much changed, and as completely whipped-out in appearance as he is."

"Don't you know?"

"Of course not, or we would not have asked you. What is the matter with him?"

"Suppose you guess."

"Is he sick?" we asked.

"No."

"Has he lost money?"

"No."

"Has he lost a member of his family?"

"No, he has gained one."

"What do you mean?"

"I mean, that he is married!"

XXI.

The Breaking of a Bruised Reed

Two evangelists were conducting a meeting in one of our large inland cities. One night the speaker of the hour had his attention drawn to the face of a woman in the audience on account of its perfectly hopeless expression. It was a fine countenance, but some kind of happening in the past had evidently stolen away the brightness, and left it with the appearance of having been turned to stone.

We have seen a smitten life in the past, whose solitariness and silence made us think somehow of waves breaking with solemn sound on lonely, barren shores; or we would have summoned up a human figure standing on a prominent headland watching the sun going down for the last time in the billows of the sea. In some such way the melancholy unexpectant face in the congregation affected us; and yet this stunned, lifeless-looking countenance belonged to a young married woman, not over twenty-four years of age.

One night as the people were going out of the church, she passed near the speaker, when in deepest pity for a sorrow-laden soul he reached out his hand and said: "God bless your heart."

In an instant a grateful flash leaped in her eyes, that strangely reminded him of the gratitude he had beheld manifested in the look of dumb brutes. He remembered a dog which he had once stooped over and patted, a poor creature that had never known anything but blows, kicks, abuse and starvation; and pitiful to relate, the wistful, appealing, grateful gaze of the dog was the same he saw in the woman.

One night she was not in her place, and on her reappearance next day he said:

"I missed you last night." And again there sprang up for just a moment the same touched look, as though so simple a speech meant much to her.

— 125 —

It seems that it is through acts of courtesy and deeds of kindness that the door of many hearts has to be opened to receive the messages of God; and so it was in the case of Evelyn G—. A glance of pity and interest where none had been expected, was the first swallow of a coming spring. It makes a great difference in the appearance of this world when we have one person in it who cares for us. And the Gospel itself has a different sound when we are not alone in life, but stand enriched and blessed with the friendship and love of others around us.

Anyhow, a door was opened somewhere in this long-shut-up life, the Spirit of God got in, and one night the young woman came to the altar. Other nights found her there, and it was evident that a terrible conflict was going on within her soul.

She asked for no counsel, sought no sympathy, reflected on nobody, but with set features and groanings of spirit rather than with the lips, she seemed to be engaged in a life and death struggle on some hidden battlefield of the heart.

One person alone knew her past life, and all unsolicited we were told by that individual a history that made the heart ache and the tears run swiftly down the face. There had been sin, but under such circumstances of girlish ignorance, innocence and betrayal of trust, that one could but wonder why the thunderbolts of justice and judgment did not fall from the skies and destroy the man who was the blighter and blaster under the guise of adviser and protector.

Nevertheless all wrongs of earth must be forgiven if we ourselves would receive the pardon of Heaven. So the day came when the broken-hearted woman forgave the injurer and placed the lifelong wound under the Blood, when with a cry of joy that penetrated and thrilled every soul in the audience she flung herself back in the arms of her mother, and with clasped hands and radiant face looked like a being just arrived from the Glory World.

In the remaining days of the meeting, it was a benediction to see her soul drinking deep at the fountain, and eating of the Gospel manna which was raining upon and around her. She had been thirsty and hungry so long! And then she had been hopeless so long! From sixteen to twenty-four she had eaten, drank, walked, slept and awoke under a cloud of impenetrable blackness. And it was growing blacker as the months rolled by! And the whisper of the Devil to commit suicide was getting louder! And her heart was becoming harder!—until the meeting came on, which brought Christ to her soul in pardon, peace, victory, and blessed salvation.

Months afterward when far away across the continent we received letters telling us of the good this woman was doing. She had taken an active interest in church work. Instead of asking for a Sunday school class, she went out on the streets and found or made one. She spent a certain portion of each day in visiting the sick and helping the poor. She divided repeatedly the little store in her purse with the needy; did it with happy tears welling up in her eyes, and then would crown the visit of mercy with a fervent, loving prayer sent direct to the Throne from a room or cabin of abject poverty.

Other letters were written telling how she had organized a mission in a neglected part of the city; and following this news came still another communication stating that she had been elected organist of the church Sunday school. Every succeeding report for a whole year was of this character, and filled the heart with thanksgiving for such a beautifully redeemed life.

Then came a long silence of months; and one day a letter arrived stating that certain lady members of the church had dug up something relative to the past history of Evelyn G— and were industriously circulating it. That when the reports first reached Mrs. G— she seemed much shocked, but went on in her duties just the same, trying to be bright and cheerful as before. But the talk had increased to such an extent that a number of the female members had dropped her socially, cut her publicly in the church work and religious services, and their victim was steadily sinking under the treatment.

Another letter several months afterward reported that the division in the church over the case of Mrs. G— had steadily increased in gravity. That various tongues kept fanning the flames and adding more fuel, as if determined to destroy the soul which Christ had saved. One report was that she had ruined a preacher's usefulness; a second that she had deceived her husband; a third that she had always been bad from girlhood, etc., etc.

The letter said that Mrs. G— never opened her lips in reply to anything or anybody; that she never struck back, but looked like a wounded fawn facing with great melancholy eyes the hunters and hounds who were seeking its death.

After this came still other tidings through which we learned that she had given up her class in Sunday school, ceased her mission work, and came very rarely to church. That when she did attend public worship she would sit in the last pew, and would leave hurriedly at the close, without speaking to a soul.

A whole year more rolled by and once again we visited the city where three years before we had witnessed a wonderful revival, and among the number saved had been made to rejoice over the remarkable case we have just described. We went promptly to the street and number where she had formerly lived, and rang the bell. A strange face appeared at the door, and to inquiries replied that Mrs. G— no longer lived there, and that none of them knew where she resided.

Going to the house of a church member in the neighborhood, we were told by that good lady that Mrs. G—'s husband had left her, and that she had gone to live with her mother in a distant part of the city, fully twenty or thirty blocks away. After taking down the address we asked:

"Does Mrs. G— ever come to church?"

"No, indeed. She has not darkened our church doors for nearly a year. She likes other places better than the House of God."

"What do you mean?" we inquired.

"I mean," replied the lady with a severely virtuous look, "that she goes to theatres on week nights, and to the parks on Sunday. The last time I heard from her, six or seven months ago, she was with a set of worldly people in the largest theatre down town."

"Poor dear heart," we said, with a big ache in our own.

"I think you are wasting pity on a very bad woman," was the rejoinder of our Christian friend.

After a moment's pause we said:

"My sister, do you remember one of the most touching descriptions in prophecy about the Saviour?"

"I don't know that I do."

"I am afraid," we returned, "that many of Christ's followers do not know it."

"What is the prophecy?" the woman asked with some interest.   *42:3, MATTHEW 12:20*

"Here it is," we replied, reading from Isaiah: " 'The bruised reed will he not break; and smoking flax will he not quench.' " Then closing the book we said: "Here is stated the exceeding tenderness of the Saviour with those who have been afflicted, injured and all but wounded to death in the battle of life. The person in his desire for goodness and heaven may not realize a flame in the heart, but have instead a mere fireless smoking that is seen in flax when drying. And yet even that feeble spiritual state the Lord will not despise. As for one who has been bruised by sin, so that a touch would break the poor reed-like character, even that one is safe with the Redeemer, for instead of crushing what is already nearly ruined by the Devil, Jesus would restore and save every such heart-broken and undone man or woman."

The lady before us was silent and solemn enough now, while we continued:

"The young woman whom the pitiless tongues in your church drove from duty and the House of God to the theatre, and back to the world, was not the bad character you thought and said she was. We know her history, and the bitter wrongs heaped upon her all through her life to this hour. She sinned, but was more sinned against than sinning. She was betrayed where she had a right to expect protection and safety. She never deceived her husband but told him all before marriage. He was a brute to her after he wedded her, but she was true to him. Neither was she the bad girl that rumor said she was. Those who know her past life best declare that she was a bright, happy, innocent girl until the disaster came upon her at sixteen. We wrote these facts to several individuals here in the midst of the tongue storm raised against her, but it seems that truth was not the thing that was wanted, but the heart-break and utter overthrow of a young woman who was trying to save her soul, do better, and gain Heaven!"

Noticing the increasingly disturbed look on our auditor's face, we added:

"The difference between Jesus Christ and your church is that He wants to save souls and you prefer to destroy them. He would mend and restore the bruised reed, while your people would break one with every opportunity. You will excuse me, my sister, in saying that your church may have Christianity, but they certainly do not possess Christ. And more than that, if your membership has religion, it is not the kind which the world wants to see, and that it must have, to lift it up from its fallen condition into light, hope, faith, salvation and a better life."

*   *   *   *   *   *

An half hour after this scene we were threading our way along some dingy streets, hunting for the childhood home of Evelyn G—. It stood, we were told, several blocks back from the river but overlooking the same as it swept with broad and majestic current towards the South.

The streets became hilly and broken, and the houses straggling, before we stood before the one we sought. The porch was dusty, the side and back yards silent and empty, and the window shutters all closed.

We rang the doorbell, but got only echoes and the barking of a distant dog for our pains. We rang again, and a plainly-dressed, tired-looking woman came to a window of the next house and said "Nobody's at home."

Coming nearer to her, we lifted our hat and asked:

"Does the mother of Mrs. G— live here?"

"Yes, sir, but she is not at home today, and hardly ever is. Pour soul, I don't wonder that she wants to get away."

"What is her trouble?" we asked, with a vague fear arising in the heart.

"It is not trouble, sir, but troubles. Her only son is in the Philippines; then her two oldest daughters are married, moved away and she hardly ever hears from them; and now the last one is gone."

"Does not Mrs. G— live here with her mother?"

"She did, sir, but she is gone now, and has been for over four months."

"Where is she?"

"Nobody knows. Some say she is in Chicago; others say New York. I don't believe that her own mother knows where she is."

A few more words were exchanged which brought no additional light, and the woman disappeared in the depths of her house.

We returned and sat down on the porch steps of Evelyn's silent and desolate home, and surrendered the mind up to reflections of the most melancholy nature.

Some children were playing in the roadway farther down the street. A dog was lazily and dreamily watching them as he was stretched upon a front gallery. The whole neighborhood in the quiet, almost pulseless afternoon air seemed asleep. Far across the wide river stretched a landscape of fields shut in by a distant range of purple hills, and beyond them a low misty line of fleecy clouds rested on the horizon.

As we looked from the doorstep upon the scene we said aloud:

"And far beyond those hills and clouds, somewhere on the face of the earth, roams Evelyn G— with a broken heart!"

Just then a hand-organ in the distance commenced playing "The Sweetest Story Ever Told." There was a swift rush of tears to the eyes, and we thought:

"Ah, well! It was sweet to her once, but it became bitter enough in a very little while. Then she tried to love again, and was struck down by hands that should have helped her. What has she to make her seek and trust human affection again? Will she ever do so again? And if she is lost at last who is most to blame! And when the judgment of God falls, will it come heaviest on the woman who tried to do right, or upon those who beat back and down a soul that was trying to quit sin, leave the world, and find its way to Christ, safety, duty, and Heaven?"

The evening came on, the children went away, and the strains of the organ had long ago ceased. We walked down to the river bank where the yellow waves broke with a solemn wash upon the shore, and looked across to where the snowy masses on the horizon had changed into an ominous thunder cloud. We reflected that on this very scene her eyes had often rested, and that as a happy, innocent girl she had many times heard these lapping waves on the shore. They remained still, but where now was the injured woman? Far from her childhood's home, and farther still from God, where was she?

And the question would keep coming up as if insisting on a definite and final answer.

"Who is most to blame, the bruised reed or those who broke the bruised reed?"

Then as if in reply memory recalled a Bible scene in which a woman figured whose history was darker than that of Evelyn G—. In that living picture of old, the guilty one had been dragged before Christ and clamor was made that she should be stoned according to the law of Moses. And then while human tongues lashed and raged around the silent and trembling victim, the Holy One who knew no sin stooped and wrote on the ground as though He heard them not. Finally He arose and said unto the accusing crowd: "He that is without sin among you, let him first cast a stone at her." And once more He stooped and traced that strange, unknown writing in the dust.

When He stood up again the accusers were all gone; and He concerning whom prophecy said He would not break a bruised reed, spoke kindly to the crushed, unhappy woman, and planted a new hope in her heart, opened up a new life before her eyes, and swung Heaven itself in front of her exultant soul in the words, "Go, and sin no more."

XXII.

A Startling Confession

A prominent minister of the Gospel once stated in his pulpit that he had listened in his Study to such ghastly life histories from desperate looking men, that more than a dozen times he had been ready to take flight from the scene, and would have done so if the narrator had made the slightest aggressive movement toward him.

In keeping with this remarkable statement, the writer can say that confessions have been made him in the past of such unusual character and dreadful nature, that he verily believes that nothing in the way of divulgence of sin and crime could now astonish him.

These revelations of a hidden and unsuspected life, were like lightning flashes illumining a dark forest teeming with creatures unseen before; or like a sudden vision into another world peopled with beings and characters unknown and unimagined up to that hour.

We have seen a stately mansion surrounded with lovely shade trees and beautified with lawn and flower gardens, and were told while admiring it that a horrible crime had been committed inside its walls. As we looked again after that shocking statement, and saw the sunlight falling lovingly upon the balustraded porch, we thought how little there was to indicate the unhappy history which had occurred within. The pigeons were cooing and skimming about the eaves, some happy voiced children attended by their nurse were playing on the lawn, while a large Newfoundland dog stood under the trees gravely and approvingly contemplating the scene. It was all so fair and peaceful, that one could scarcely credit the dark tragedy which had been enacted there only a few months previous, and yet a double murder of a most frightful and unnatural character had been committed in that place.

Equally startling have we been to find that the grave, quiet, dignified man in the audience was an escaped convict, and that the innocent looking woman with a girlish face had three living husbands, and was stained with an awful crime besides.

From these things we gather that we know very little of what is transpiring behind the walls of our neighbor's house; and next to nothing about the people who jostle us on the street, and sit by us on the car and in the church. It is only now and then we get a flash which lights up the woods, and we see a panther lying on the limb of a tree, a scorpion on a log, and a snake coiled up under a bush by the side of the narrow path where we are walking. Or, to change the figure, a door or window blind is suddenly opened, and we mark faces and forms all unknown to the street and undreamed of by us until that moment.

At a certain camp meeting in the South, one of the preachers in a sermon at night held up the dreadfulness of concealed iniquity. The discourse fell upon the ears of a profoundly awed and conscience smitten audience, although there was but little outward demonstration at the altar. It seemed that a number shrank from coming forward after such a fearful delineation, lest such a movement would be to spot and mark themselves as acknowledged criminals and violators of law in the grossest sense.

Next morning the writer was in his tent, engaged in preparation for the morning sermon, while the Testimony meeting was in progress at the Tabernacle about an hundred feet away. Suddenly a shriek of agony, ascending from the place of worship, literally rent the air. The scream came from a woman, and we knew from the shocked, horror-stricken accent that whoever gave it was a heart-broken person. We scarcely ever heard a cry which so deeply moved us. It carried its own misery with it, and the listener could not but respond in spirit to nature's wail over the incoming of a colossal sorrow.

After this startling interruption there was a profound silence of an half hour, and then came the sound of the people leaving the Tabernacle and their scattering along the tent-lined streets. Glancing out, we saw that all were talking earnestly and knew that they were discussing the incident of that morning.

Recognizing a gentleman, we called him aside and asked why the woman had given that fearful scream. He replied, "Her husband made a confession this morning," and then related the circumstance.

It seemed that this husband, whose name was D, was one of the convicted ones in the audience of the night before. Next morning he accompanied his wife to the Experience meeting, to her great joy, as she fancied she saw in his gloomy face signs of conviction, the natural precursor of salvation.

He took his seat just behind her, and after a number had testified, he arose to his feet as pale as death, and with a faltering voice said,

"I have kept a load of guilt on my heart for thirty long years. I cannot stand it any longer. It is killing me by inches. I want to say here before everybody, that just after the close of the war I killed a man!"

Whether he intended to say more or not we do not know, for just as these last words were uttered, the wife gave the agonized cry we heard in the tent, and fell upon the ground at the feet of her husband unconscious.

Something of the shock may be imagined, when the thought rushed over her:

"The father of my children is a murderer! The man with whom I have been most intimate on earth, who has gone with me through life side by side, has his hands red with the blood of a fellow creature!"

No wonder she went down senseless in the dust.

We next asked our informant where the woman was and was told that she had been born to an adjacent room by sympathizing friends. Our following question was, "Where is the man?" and the reply was, "He has gone to his tent."

In a few minutes we found him there, lying on a cot and looking more like a dead than a living man. Taking a camp stool by his side we laid our hand upon his and found it cold and clammy, while his body was trembling as with a chill. With a heart full of pity, we said:

"My brother, are you not glad that you made a clean breast of your guilt today?"

Turning a pair of despairing eyes upon us he answered:

"Mr. C., the law will hang me."

"Hang or no hang," we replied, "are you not glad that you have gotten that black stuff out of your heart which has been weighing it down for thirty years?"

Grasping our hand, and with a look of unspeakable relief upon his face, he said in a firm, manly tone:

"God in heaven knows that I am."

*   *   *   *   *   *

It is not necessary to dwell on other particulars of the case occurring at this immediate time. Suffice it to say that D. went home, submitted to arrest, was cast into jail, and underwent his trial.

The Scripture plainly teaches that when we do what God bids us, He will take us up, fight our battles and deliver us from all our trouble. This was what took place with D. The Lord touched the heart of judge and jury; moved on men here and there; brought first one thing and then another to pass, and completely delivered the man.

The words of the Psalmist could have been truly appropriated and repeated by him in description of what had been done for him and in him: "He hath delivered my soul from death, mine eyes from tears and my feet from falling." There was a strange literal fulfillment of the verse in his case. His feet did not fall through the trap door of the scaffold; his eyes were saved from weeping through the pardoning and consoling love of Christ, and his spirit as well as body were not given over unto death, but were both brought forth from imprisonment and bondage, into life and liberty according to the promise of the Almighty.

Such was the man's gratitude for the salvation of his soul while in prison, and for the rescue of his life from the law soon after, that he would not wait for the next camp meeting to obtain holiness of heart, but sought the blessing at once, and months before the regular annual encampment he had swept into Beulah Land and was one of the strong ones in Canaan when we next beheld him.

Repeatedly the writer and his Singer met this doubly redeemed man during the camp which followed the one mentioned in the beginning of this sketch, and we both had to admit that among the bright, restful faces we beheld in the meeting, that the most peaceful one of all was that of the man who the year before had made such a startling and terrible confession.

XXIII.

The History of a Prayer

In a small town in Kentucky lived a godly woman by the name of Mary M.,[1] whose heart was greatly burdened for the salvation of the people in her community. Very often in secret she poured out, with tears, her petition that God would send the place a sweeping revival of New Testament pattern and power. It is the biography of this prayer which forms the body of this sketch, and a most remarkable history it was.

We gather from the Bible that God hearkens to our requests, and is pledged to answer them if offered in the right spirit, and we will abide in faith and faithfulness. One other condition, however, is clearly exacted of Heaven, and that is that the time of fulfillment be left in the hands of the Lord.

Several facts make this understanding to be imperative. One alone which we mention is sufficient to satisfy any reasonable mind, viz., the moral freedom of people with whom God has to work in order to answer the petition. The angel told Daniel that he had been hindered three weeks in coming to him, by the Prince of the Kingdom of Persia. This Prince in his opposition brings out at once in the most vivid manner the stubbornness, ignorance, prejudice, sinfulness and spirit liberty itself which so often stand in between us, and the coming messenger and message of relief and gladness sent us from the skies. In a word, hindrances still exist to our reception of what we are told in the Word we can properly pray for as a comfort and blessing to our own life and that of others.

In view of the things desired, and the mental and moral constitution of men, God tells us to "wait on Him," to "patiently wait," and the promise is that He will bring, what we plead for, to pass.

1. MARY McAFEE. (SEE PAGE 72 OF H.C. MORRISON'S BOOK, "REMARKABLE CONVERSIONS."

If ever a woman had need to exercise faith it was Mary M., after she begged God with strong cries and tears for the revival. For years there was not a sign that the petition had even been noticed by heaven.

True it was, that a long while after several preachers confessed that during those very years they were deeply moved to hold a meeting in the town where this woman supplicator lived, but they allowed the impression to pass away. The solitary pleader for the community however, did not know this, and so kept on in her praying under an obviously impenetrable sky, and to a God who did not seem to hear, and certainly did not answer.

In the Bible we read that when the Lord could not find a prophet in Israel to carry a message of rebuke and warning to His idolatrous people, He reached His hand down in Judah and brought forth a man of God from that country to do His will.

In like manner there was a scarcity of human instruments in the land where Mary M. lived, and God looked around in vain to find a man who would bear a message to the town of S.,[2] which would make that community to sigh and weep over its sins, and cause at the same time his daughter, who had mourned so long, to cease her crying and go to rejoicing over the fulfillment of her often uttered supplication.

So the divine eye was turned in the Judah direction, and the divine hand began to prepare other instruments outside of the town of S. and beyond its county boundaries, and far from the state itself, who were to bring salvation to the people and prove to that grieving servant of His that God was still, as He has always been, One who not only hears but also answers prayer.

In the State of Mississippi and removed from S. by fully six hundred miles, was a young preacher named H.[3] who was hungry for full salvation, but did not entirely understand the nature of his own longing. He prayed much, and even agonized, but there was no Philip passing along this desert portion of his life to ask him as he read and supplicated if he understood his own reading and prayers. No Ananias came into those days of spiritual bewil-

2. STANFORD, KENTUCKY
3. REV. W. W. HOPPER

derment and at times blindness and darkness, with the command to arise, and be filled with the Holy Ghost.

While H. was in this state of mind, a newspaper reporter in the city of Louisville wrote a brief sketch or religious item about a holy woman who lived, as he stated, in a small town in the hill country of Kentucky. He mentioned several things concerning her, making in all an ordinary sized paragraph. But little as it was, it held in its narrow limits, in a strange way, the sanctification of the Mississippi preacher, and the long prayed for revival at S.

Many thousand copies of that issue of the paper, the Courier-Journal, were scattered over the country and lost to view forever. But one sheet of the publication God determined should survive the general destruction. It fluttered South, and like a Messenger Bird as it proved, nestled in the hand and under the eye of H. Carelessly glancing down its columns the preacher read the following words:

"There lives in S., Kentucky, a woman named Mary M. She dwells in a small yellow cottage in the edge of the town and keeps the Toll Gate. She claims to have been sanctified, and—"

This was all he read, but it was all God wanted him to see, and was all indeed that he needed. Like Eleazar when he recognized the hand of the Lord in confirmatory providences which guided him on his way to secure Rebecca for Isaac, so H. stood thrilled, and worshiped God as he felt that in a bit of printed paper he had beheld the directing finger of Heaven.

He said to himself, "That is just what I need. I want to be sanctified."

In his case the instructing Philip was six hundred miles away, and if interview was to be had he would have to seek it, and be the traveler. Distance, however, was not the only drawback, but the lack of funds to meet railroad expenses stared him in the face.

This naturally brought forth the prayer, "Lord, if this thing is from You, and You desire me to see that woman and obtain instruction from her, grant that the means necessary for the trip will be provided."

In a week's time, a railroad pass and money necessary for incidental expenses were placed in his hands without any hint or solicitation on his part.

A few days later this seeker after truth alighted from the train at the place of destination and asked for the "yellow cottage" at the Toll Gate. Knocking at the door he inquired if Mary M. lived there, and was answered in the affirmative. Invited in the house he told her what he had come for, and as it did not take Holiness people long to enter upon business, the faithful woman and her sister began to instruct him in the way of the Lord "more perfectly," and in a few minutes were pleading mightily in prayer in his behalf, while he himself wept and prayed and groaned upon the floor.

On the second or third day the fire fell, the long-desired blessing of sanctification swept into the emptied and completely consecrated soul, and H., full of joy and the Holy Ghost, was on his way back to Mississippi.

It was after this that the writer began to hear much of H. Of course he was misunderstood by his congregation, and Conference, and so became acquainted very soon with the "Fiery Furnace," and obtained a great deal of positive light on the history and experience of Shadrach, Meshach and Abednego. He also received a kind mental geographical chart of the Island of Patmos with a marvelous amount of insight into the life of the famous exile on that wave-washed and solitary shore, a man who had been sent there on account of the Word of God, and the testimony of Jesus Christ! We heard that he was "clear off," "a fanatic," "usefulness ended," etc., etc. But at the same time we were informed that he had constant revivals wherever he went. We do not know at this time of spiritual greenness and ignorance in our life, how we reconciled the two reports. Perhaps we did not try to harmonize them. The thing was high, and we had not then attained unto it.

One rumor reached us that he, H., while preaching a great convicting sermon, had thrown a chair off the platform. Of course, to some who had never knocked the devil out of their church, nor kicked a sin out of their lives, nor hurled a sinner into the kingdom of heaven, all this was perfectly dreadful. In fact, it was the unpardonable sin. Preachers could smoke their cigars and pipes, church members could break the Sabbath and tell impure stories, and all that could be readily overlooked. But for a man to overturn a chair in the sacred pulpit, while illustrating some truth under the power of the Spirit; Oh, that was fearful! terrible! sacrilegious! and not to be forgiven in this world nor in the world to come!

At a session of an annual conference several members became exceedingly violent on the floor toward H. Two were especially bitter. One of them, turning towards the quiet-looking, peaceful-faced victim, shook his finger at him and vociferated to the chairman:

"Bishop, I would rather the devil from hell should preach on my circuit than that man!"

The editor of a Christian Advocate, who afterwards became a Bishop, was present during this stormy and heart-sickening scene. His eyes, with the gaze of many others, rested upon the accused man; and in commenting upon the occurrence when all was over, he said:

"The face of H. was the quietest and most peaceful in the entire Conference!"

Soon after the scene related, H. was fairly driven by ecclesiastical pressure to take refuge in a distant Western Conference. The Spirit, however, followed him, and so, wherever he went, revivals sprang up and salvation flowed.

One or more years passed away in this manner, when opposition similar to that from which he had fled became so great in the West that he turned back homeward once more.

At this time we heard again of him. It was the same old story of revivals and opposition, and opposition and revivals.

The man seemed to be on the best terms with God, but somehow he could not please his brethren in the ministry.

Meanwhile the writer, *BEVERLY CARRADINE,* as pastor of a large city church, was hungry for something in the spiritual life that he did not know the name of, nor its exact nature. He was conscious at this period of desiring two things very ardently; one was a satisfying blessing for his own soul, and second a great, gracious, old-time, old-fashioned, Wesleyan, Apostolic, Scriptural Revival in his Church, *THE CARONDELET STREET METHODIST CHURCH IN NEW ORLEANS.*

While praying about the matter and mentally casting about for human help, the face of H. was quietly and steadily presented to his mind with an unmistakable impression, "Send for him."

The invitation was forwarded, the invited came, and the meeting opened. The power of God fell on the fourth day. In the eight days' meeting, one hundred souls were converted, twenty-five sanctified, and four young men entered the ministry.

While listening to the third sermon of H. the writer suddenly saw not only the possibility but the actuality of the Second Work of Grace. He promptly bowed at the altar, came six times, and, after a complete consecration, unquestioning faith in the Word of God, and three days of almost continuous prayer, one morning at 9 o'clock, on June 1, 1889, the Baptism with the Holy Ghost and Fire fell upon, filled and literally overwhelmed him!

All this may appear irrelevant to the subject of this sketch. It may seem that not only God had overlooked Mary M., but we, her biographer, had also forgotten her. But so far from this being the case, the circumstances just related made the highway along which was to come the long-deferred blessings of heaven to S. God was preparing servants to bring the message of gladness to the heart of Mary M., who had been praying faithfully and persistently for ten years for the community she loved and in which she lived.

Four years passed away after the writer received the Baptism with the Holy Ghost, which were spent by him in city pastorates. Meantime Mary M. prayed on for the town of S.

Finally we entered the evangelistic work, and began to circle about the nation. After almost a year had been thus spent, the pastor of Mary M., a devout man, suddenly felt impressed to write to us to hold a meeting in his church. We accepted the call and came. Whereupon a gifted editor-evangelist said in his epigrammatic and culminating way: "When C. jumped off the train one morning with his valise in his hand, the revival had come!"

What need to speak of that revival, which has gone already into the history of the holiness movement? Suffice it to say that the power of God fell upon the people; that salvation rolled; that the meeting had to be moved twice to obtain larger quarters; that the brass band of a traveling troupe played in vain in front of the theater to secure an audience; not a dozen came; while at the largest church in town the people filled the seats, jammed the vestibule and aisles, crowded the chancel, lined the altar rail and sat on the floor of the pulpit to hear the Word of God, while scores and scores, with tears, laughter, shouts and clapping of hands, were swept into reclamation, regeneration and entire sanctification.

The revival had come!

The prayer of Mary M., ascending for fifteen long years, had been heard at last!

XXIV.

A Miracle of Grace

In one of our largest cities a man whom we shall call Dunlap led for years the life of a criminal. He had a large, muscular body, a great, massive head, and a will power bigger than both combined. He was a bold, bad man and stopped short of nothing in the accomplishment of his burglaries, which were usually planned on an extensive scale, and seemed to be enjoyed by him just in proportion to their danger and difficulty.

Walls were scaled, doors and windows entered, bolts snapped and big iron safes burst open before the crowbar, chisel and dynamite of this fearless individual.

Policemen had a wholesome dread of the man, and never dreamed of attacking him single-handed. Detectives dogged his steps, and every effort was made to so overtake and fasten guilt upon him as to land their victim in the penitentiary. But successful as he was fearless, and cunning as he was bold, it was fully ten years before the trap was sprung, and Dunlap, caught in one of his store robberies, was overpowered by numbers and dragged to jail.

He had been incarcerated a number of weeks awaiting his trial, when one day some godly women who made a practice of visiting the prisons in the city on the Sabbath passed his cell and handed him a newspaper containing D. L. Moody's sermon on Justification by Faith.

The prisoner, more from the tediousness of the solitary confinement than anything else, took up the printed sheet and commenced reading. Suddenly his eyes fell upon the words that God would forgive the vilest criminal and foulest sinner on earth if he would simply look to and believe on His Son Jesus Christ. Then came the Scripture confirming the statement, "Being justified by faith, we have peace with God."

DWIGHT LYMAN MOODY (1837 MASS — 1899 MASS).

It would be simply impossible to describe the actual shock of astonishment that came over Dunlap as he read these words. It was like a lightning flash in his mental and spiritual world. The Spirit poured in light on the Word, and in the man as he sat reading and rereading the transfigured words with a great voiceless wonder in heart and mind.

Though the personages and periods were widely different and separated as to character and time, yet the same thing was taking place in his case that occurred to Luther when climbing up the Sacred Stairway in Rome in search after pardon. The reader will remember that as the monk was two-thirds up the steps on his knees, the Holy Ghost impressed this passage on his mind while streaming a flood of light upon it—"The just shall live by faith!"

In an instant Martin Luther saw the truth, grasped it, leaped to his feet and rushed down the staircase a converted man, to electrify the church and Europe with the restored doctrine that men are not saved by works, but by faith in the Son of God.

In a similar manner the light came upon the lonely prisoner, and as he read and reread the Bible passage, God helping him, he grasped the truth with a thrill of amazement, and, looking to Jesus was, in an instant, soundly converted to God.

Of course this made a great stir in the prison, and especially outside among the people of God who heard of it. Some there were who doubted, but the man's remarkable change in face, conversation, spirit and life left no question with the Christian workers who saw him that he had been truly regenerated.

A few weeks after the prisoner's conversion, under the instruction of the Holiness Band who visited the jail, he was led into the experience of entire sanctification.

Here was another miracle of grace, and caused additional wonder with some, and increased gladness among the people of God.

As the day for the trial of his case drew near, the conviction was general that the sentence would be for a long term in the penitentiary. And because of the changed nature of the man this certainty of the coming verdict intensified sympathy in his behalf.

Dunlap had been assigned a lawyer by the judge, and this gentleman, conceiving a warm interest in his unfortunate client, gave a faithful study to the case.

One day he made an important discovery and went at once to the jail to interview the prisoner. After taking his seat in the cell, he said:

"Mr. Dunlap, I have made a very important discovery in your case which may result in my being able to get you off clear."

"Indeed," replied Dunlap. "I am glad to hear that."

"Yes," resumed the lawyer; "I find that through a technical error, as we call it, I can get you free. But in order to use my advantage I will have to obtain your consent to make a statement that is not exactly in accord with facts."

"I do not understand you," replied the prisoner, turning a steady, searching look upon the man of law.

"I mean," said his counsel, "that I will have to get you to stretch the truth a little."

"Do you mean that I must tell a falsehood?" asked Dunlap.

"Well," returned the lawyer, "if you insist in putting it in that strong way, you may do so."

"Do I understand you to say," asked Dunlap, "that my deliverance from a long term in the penitentiary depends upon my telling an untruth—in other words a lie?"

"Well, yes; that is about the sum of the matter."

"Then," answered Dunlap, "I prefer to go to the penitentiary!"

If the man's conversion created surprise, the last occurrence increased the amazement, and Dunlap became a standing wonder among many, while Christians rejoiced over the steadfastness and faithfulness of the new convert.

According to the Bible, it is when a man meets the conditions that God requires, and turns himself over entirely to the divine keeping, that the Lord works not only mightily for him on the inside, but achieves marvelously for him on the outside.

Without being able to enter into the history of the matter, we can only say in the brief compass of this chapter that the same God who caused an angel to unlock the prison doors for Peter did likewise for the subject of this sketch, and Dunlap after a few months' incarceration walked out a pardoned and liberated man.

He speedily joined the church, secured work down in the city, and entered upon a new life in every sense of the word.

There were many, of course, who did not believe in him, and suspected a deep trick and scheme underneath the whole occurrence. Notably this was the opinion of the police and detective force. For years they kept a hawk's eye upon him, and shadowed day and night the great burly fellow who with clear, honest eyes and bright, happy face, trudged the streets of the city.

It was not long before Dunlap secured a deputyship at the Court House. The men there were not sorry to obtain the services of an individual of such physical strength and courage; and, having perfect confidence in his redeemed life, they entrusted him with large sums of money.

It was especially on these collecting days that the police and detectives would watch Dunlap, and he, not slow to perceive this, went on his happy, tranquil way, saying to a friend: "They don't know I carry a treasure in my heart that all the money of this city is not able to buy. I would be a fool indeed to part with what I've got for the few hundred dollars I gather in my collecting tours."

As a church member Dunlap was regular in his attendance, and prompt in payment of money to meet the pastoral and conference claims. In addition to this, he would put aside a small amount each month from his salary, in order to attend a Holiness Camp Meeting that was located about two hundred miles from the city. This was his solitary recreation. He said he needed no other, and cared for no other.

About this time the writer was sent as pastor to the church where Dunlap held his membership. One of the first things the redeemed man said about the new preacher was:

"Now I need not go off to a camp meeting for soul food. God has sent me a Holiness preacher, and I can have full salvation preaching without taking an expensive trip to hear it. So from this time I will give as an extra amount to the church that which I took before to pay for my camp meeting trip."

After a year's pastorate the writer was sent from that church where he had been stationed to another in the same city. In leading a farewell prayer meeting of four or five hundred people, he advised them not to follow him, but remain where they were and stand by their new pastor. With a few more concluding words of direction and counsel, he sat down. There was a profound silence for a few moments, when Dunlap arose and, with a voice choked with emotion, said:

"All may stay here that will, but I am going to heaven by way of First Church."

The church he alluded to was the charge just given to the writer. And here he promptly presented himself on the next Sabbath and was the first accession of the seven hundred and fifty who flocked to that place of worship as new members.

One day we were visiting the home of Dunlap, when in the course of conversation he said:

"Would you like to see two photographs of myself taken at different times?"

We replied that we would, when he went to a wardrobe and from a drawer within brought out two pictures. Handing the first one to us he said:

"This was taken while I was in the service of the Devil, and when he had me bound hand and foot."

As we looked upon the face on the cardboard we could scarcely keep back an expression of disgust. The bloated countenance was not only marked heavily with lines of sin, but was so grossly animal as to arouse in the heart a sense of loathing and in the mind a feeling almost of horror.

He saw the look, and with a smile laid the other photograph before us, saying:

"This one was taken since I entered the service of Christ."

As we gazed upon the fine, open, shining face in the picture, it fairly staggered faith in one's own eyesight and judgment to believe that these two portraits were of the same man.

Looking up at Dunlap with an expression of wonder, we saw the tears dripping down his face.

With our own eyes wet, and a husky sound in the voice we said to the deeply moved man:

"Brother Dunlap, you could not preach the Gospel more powerfully and effectively than to carry these two photographs around with you and show them to the people. They constitute a Gospel and an unanswerable argument in themselves."

His reply was:

"I have done so many times, and said as I showed first one, and then the other, 'This is what the Devil brought me to, and this is what Jesus did for me!' And I have never known it to fail to convict the person who heard what I said and looked at the pictures I showed him."

Dunlap has been dead for several years; but though in heaven he still speaks on earth in the memories of men. And if recollection of him should perish, the two pictures that are left would still proclaim what the Devil does in the way of moral ruin and degradation, and what the Son of God can do for the vilest and most sinful of men in the way of recovery and full salvation.

XXV.

The Last Warning

The Bible, history and observation as well, agree as to the facts of warnings being sent to individuals who were rushing towards and bordering upon destruction. In some instances they were numerous, and in others but a single one could be recalled. But whether frequent or rare there would necessarily be in each case what we call in the caption of this sketch "The Last Warning."

A Pharaoh is told by Moses that he is receiving his final call to do right from heaven. A Paul brings a farewell message to Felix. An angel stands before Balaam with a waving sword. A David with his harp is providentially placed before King Saul to divert his mind from gloom and his life from ruin. The Christ Himself stands before Pilate as the remaining opportunity of that Ruler to decide for the truth and escape the destruction which finally came upon him.

In illustration of the same fact, we see in history a person thrusting a note in the hand of Caesar which if read would have saved him from the daggers of Casca and Brutus. And could we but know a little part of this kind of history going on around us, and put it in book form, it would be the most profoundly absorbing of earthly volumes.

Of course after dreadful events have taken place, and fearful ends have been met, people find it easy to remember certain strange circumstances that transpired then, which they now most distinctly remember and also recall having remarked upon at the time as a warning sent from the other world, etc., etc.

But leaving the rambling of these after-date prophets out, the truth remains that the Almighty in recognition of the unspeakable value of a human soul, and seeing the approaching peril and coming death of that being, will work unusually and startlingly to arouse the spirit from its carelessness and sinfulness, and save the man from present and everlasting disaster.

It is true that the admission of this very fact opens the door to error; and Superstition luxuriates in this realm, translating the note of the hovering owl, the crow of the cock and the prolonged howl of a dog at night into omens of imminent distress and death. But leaving out all the creations of fancy, we have such an abundance of facts left as to make the most thoughtless and unconcerned to be burdened and troubled.

The truth is that a pitiful God does try to save men who are nearing the grave and a lost world; and that this fact also necessarily embraces the other, that there comes to all such persons the last one of that mystic number of warnings.

If men who have felt the stirrings of the Spirit could but know that at some moment in their lives God was moving, resisting, striving and speaking for the last time, how full of horror it seems to us they would be.

We have listened to the deep-toned bell of a great steamboat on the Mississippi as first the minutes and then the moments of departure drew near. A quarter of an hour before leaving there are nine strokes of the bell; ten minutes later three; and just at starting one! As that last solemn peal rings out, the rope is cast off, the plank drawn in, the wheels plunged into the foaming water, and the boat is gone. In this illustration it is to be observed that while the warnings are ample, yet they lessen in number as the moment of departure draws near.

The analogy could be strikingly drawn in the case of the doomed man. The calls from heaven and earth have not been lacking; but their decreasing number and power is the alarming feature of the case.

When a man is beheld rushing upon a great, unseen peril, it is a human custom to multiply shouts and cries accompanied with unlimited wavings of hands and signals of danger. On the part of Heaven it is just the other way. The number of calls and efforts to save seem to lessen like the bell tolling nine, then three, and the final melancholy knell-like one.

They also decrease in power. This last fact arises from the blunting and deadening of spiritual sensibility through long resistance to the voice, touch, and actual strugglings of the Spirit. The man by his own acts has put himself where he cannot hear the message, feel the hand, or recognize the divine effort in his behalf.

A person near him says something about the Ides of March, but he does not understand. The note is thrust into his hand to remain unread. People near him speak of somebody being in great danger; he wonders whom they are talking about. In a Gospel meeting he has a dim consciousness of a preacher saying something about the Dead Line in the Bible, and God's last call. But he does not know whom he is referring to, and the faint impression soon passes away.

And yet when the minister was uttering the sentence so meaningless and idle to him, the last toll of the bell was being sounded. Another Moses had said thou shalt hear from God no more, and had left a hardened man to a coming destruction which was to be as sudden and overwhelming as the Red Sea was to the king of Egypt.

One of these occurrences remains with the writer as vividly today as at the time of its happening a number of years ago.

The closing service of a certain camp meeting had arrived. The audience was large, and the preacher of the evening was delivering a sermon of wonderful solemnity and heart-searching power. The writer sat on the platform with other ministers, in a great spirit travail that God would bless the closing appeal and save many souls.

To this hour he recalls the stillness of that summer night, the glimmering of the stars through the trees, the song of the katydids in the woods, and the voice of the speaker as he pled with sinners to be saved. Those sights and sounds have become strangely interblended and associated, forming together a picture never to be forgotten of that memorable occasion.

In the congregation sat a young man who gave less attention than anyone else to what was being said from the pulpit, and yet he of all others should have drunk in every word of the sermon,

IDES: IN THE ROMAN CALENDAR, THE 15TH OF MARCH, MAY, JULY, AND OCTOBER, AND THE 13TH OF ALL THE OTHER MONTHS. ACCORDING TO PLUTARCH (PLOUTARCHOS) (≈ 46 – ≈ 120), A GREEK BIOGRAPHER, JULIUS CAESAR (100 BC – 44 BC) IGNORED A SOOTHSAYER'S WARNING TO BEWARE THE IDES OF MARCH, THE DAY ON WHICH HE WAS SLAIN.

and acted more promptly on the invitation to come at once to Christ, because he was receiving his last warning. Could he but have known that in less than two hours he would be millions of miles away in a distant world, lost and forever undone, how he would have stopped the preacher by cries of agony as he fell backward in his seat, or down upon his face at the altar.

But the Ides had come and he did not know it. The bell was tolling one, and he did not hear it. With persistent attempt to disturb the worship and draw others away with himself into misdoing, he whispered, laughed, or gazed vacantly at the man of God in the pulpit.

Meantime the few minutes left him on earth were fast passing away; and now as the preacher concluded his discourse, only a short hour intervened between him and the end of his probation on earth forever. Just a little way up the future, not quite sixty minutes; and now as the hymn ended only fifty; and as the prayer ceased, exactly forty, a corpse was lying outstretched on the ground two miles from the campground with a bullet hole in the forehead, and that death wound made all unwittingly by the hand of a friend. If he could have bent over and peered into the face of the motionless form before him, he would have discovered to his horror that the dead man lying there under the stars was himself!

END OF CASE 1

START OF CASE 2   In perfect harmony with what has been written in this sketch comes another occurrence of kindred nature which transpired in a Southern State. We give it as related by a Methodist preacher.

There lived in a town where he was stationed as pastor a physician who was a moral blight to the community by reason of his skeptical views and sinful life. His influence was especially baneful among the young men, some of whom he led to embrace infidelity, and a greater number to become openly and shamelessly wicked.

One Sabbath morning the preacher felt deeply impressed to preach from Proverbs 29:1: "He that being often reproved, hardeneth his neck, shall suddenly be destroyed, and that without remedy." His subject was the swift and terrible judgments of God upon those who resisted His calls and warnings.

While opening up his discourse and in the act of glancing over the audience he was profoundly surprised to see the infidel doctor sitting in the congregation. No one had ever beheld him, or even heard of his attending a church before. So there was not only genuine wonder with the pastor, but among the people at the man's presence among them.

When first observed he was about two-thirds of the way back towards the door, and in the following peculiar position: His body was bent forward with his chin resting on his hands that were folded one on top of the other, and laid on the edge of the bench immediately in front of him. He had raven hair, a heavy mustache of the same color, and coal black eyes which he fixed steadily upon the minister in the pulpit. As the preacher proceeded with his discourse, enlarging upon the calamities that befell men who strove with and against God, the big mustache would curl and the teeth gleam for a moment under the incredulous smile of the infidel. The whole mocking face seemed to say, "Do you think you can frighten me with that kind of talk? Do you imagine for a moment that I believe what you are saying?"

The preacher said that he could scarcely go on with his sermon, the man's appearance was so infernal, and his presence so paralyzing. He added that he never gazed upon a face that seemed as Satanic. The horrible thought took possession of him and could not be shaken off that the Devil was in the man and looking at him through his eyes, and mocking him through his hell-surrendered countenance.

To all appearance the preacher was the more troubled of the two, and the skeptic was having the best of the situation so far as mental burden and spiritual distress were concerned. And yet at the same time, and all unconscious of the fact, the doctor was hearing his last warning; and he was receiving it from the lips of the very man whom he was jeering at in his heart, and scorning with every line of his sinister face and position of the defiant body.

When the sermon was finished, the doctor walked out of the church, mounted his horse and rode away. Meantime the congregation scattered to their homes, while a few of the stewards remained standing by the door conversing with the pastor.

While thus engaged, suddenly the sharp report of a rifle or pistol rang out on the air from some point several hundred yards distant down the road. All were surprised at the sound and commented on its unusualness on a Sabbath morning and near a quiet country town like their own. They had, however, dismissed the thought, and were speaking of some church matter of common interest, when they saw a man running up the road towards them and crying out, "The Doctor's killed! The Doctor's killed!"

Hurrying back with him they found the loosened horse browsing on the grass, and close by, lying stone dead on the ground was the doctor with his face upturned to the sky, his black eyes wide open and staring aloft, as if he was watching the flight of his lost soul as it sped on its way to the Judgment Bar of that God whom he had resisted and grieved and insulted up to the last hour of his life.

A bullet shot from a thicket had entered the back of the skull and came out through the forehead, producing instant death. The victim evidently did not see his murderer, nor is he known until this day.

The man led a wicked life, and died as he lived, just as most people do, according to the Bible and history, and our own observation. What possessed him to visit the church that Sabbath no one ever knew. His contemptuous face and manner showed that it was for no good.

The last passage from the Bible ever read and repeated in his presence, was, "He that being often reproved, hardeneth his neck, shall suddenly be destroyed, and that without remedy." His death warrant and doom were read in his hearing and he did not know it. He crossed the Dead line and did not realize it. The last warning had come, been delivered, tarried and gone; and he to whom it was sent, was oblivious of its arrival and ignorant of its departure. The bell which had sounded nine times in his youth, and three times in his manhood, now tolled its final melancholy note of one, and the man arose, and went forth according to the words of the Book he despised, to a death that was sudden and to a destruction without remedy.

XXVI.

The Upward Look

We do not know the exact location of the soul in the body, but we are perfectly convinced that it is there. Especially is the thoughtful observer impressed with its nearness to or intimate connection with the face. By an invisible network of spiritual ropes, cords, wires, rods, wheels, cranks and pulleys, the soul from within operates the facial machinery, declaring not only its presence, but signaling by every straight, curved or quivering line in the countenance, and every changing light and shadow, and every shifting expression on brow and lip, and in the eye, the whole inner life of the spirit, with past regret, present determination and future intention, so that no manuscript reads clearer, and no book presents plainer print.

It is this strange phenomenon, which after all is nothing but the working of law, that the impostor, deceiver and sinner in general has to continually plan for and guard against. It is this that the statesman and politician has to meet with artificial methods, the manufacture of a false face and the thorough schooling of the betraying eye and tongue. And it is this same tell tale face that good people have to subdue and train to keep concealed private griefs and sacred histories which the public has no right to know.

In this countenance volume we have noticed three distinct looks that could be called the upward, the downward and the straightforward. The downward gaze is the peculiar property of sin. A guilty soul draws the head earthward. All of us have felt it who have sinned, and marked it in others who had and were transgressing. It is the common attitude in the criminal dock, and always takes place when a man has crime fastened upon him in the presence of others. The face in obedience to law is hidden by the hand or bowed before the shocked scrutiny of an assembly.

The straightforward look belongs to the innocent, honest and honorable character. It meets a fellow creature's eyes, firmly, calmly and kindly, in perfect consciousness of having done no wrong to the one before him. It is remarkable what convincing power is in this quiet, gentle, steady look.

The upward glance is the peculiar property of the heart cleansed by the power of God. In the prayer of the true worshipper it is felt to be the natural attitude; in soul rapture it is the invariable position; while in books and on the canvas the pictures of the saints always show them with the heaven bent gaze.

In the painting representing the Temptation, the artist has caught this idea, and while the countenance of Satan is lowered, the face of Christ is uplifted.

We have been repeatedly struck with the sacredness of this moral realm, as indicated by the face and eyes. It belongs to the spiritually clean. No other people can live in this country. One has to possess the character to abide there. A man may attempt it, but has to emigrate in a hurry if he has not been divinely cleansed.

We have seen the man with the downward face, invade the straightforward look region, in an attempt to bluster, bluff and deceive the people with his brazen forehead and bold, staring, defiant eyes; but we have never known one of this order to attempt the upward gaze.

We have observed another class of people endeavoring to cast the upward glance of silent worship, rapt contemplation and soul ecstasy, but as they say in the musical and oratorical world, it fell flat, and only created amusement. The upward look is not a belonging of the merely correct and moral man; it is part of the estate of the person and character who has met God, been forgiven of every sin, and thrilled with the gift of a heart made new and clean by the blood of Jesus Christ and the power of the Holy Ghost.

It is very evident, then, that excellent as is the straight vision, the upward contemplation is the better. The first declares proper relations with earth, but the second reveals a perfect adjustment and harmony with heaven. The one may stand for common honor and honesty, while the second is the sign of redemption and purity. One means clean hands, and the other a clean soul. With this light on it, we can understand what was in the mind and heart of a woman we once heard testify in a private circle. She said, "For two years since obtaining a clean heart I have felt a continual desire to look upward. I am willing for God to know every thought and desire of my life. My inmost soul is always open to Him; and many times each day I find myself looking up to Him, with a joy and exultation that I have no words to describe."

Of course we do not mean to say that the upward glance exists independently of the other. It necessarily includes the other. It is from the first, through the second, that we reach the third. A man must get right with his brother or fellow creature, before he can find harmony with God. Many in the very act of rectifying matters on the human and earthly side, are fairly electrified with an instantaneous and unspeakably glorious adjustment on the divine and heavenly side.

In illustration of the leading thought of this sketch we give the following incident which took place in the city where the writer resides:

Among the dozen or so Methodist preachers located in the metropolis, was one who was greatly given to pastoral work. His great victories were not in the pulpit, but about the firesides, and in the stores and shops of his parishioners.

In the membership of Brother L. was a devoted Christian woman, married to a man in the liquor business. Her husband's occupation was a source not only of profound mortification to her, but agony as well, as she thought of the harm he was doing to the community and the danger he himself was in, before God.

Hoping to influence him for good, she persuaded a pastor who preceded L. to take her husband into the church. And there the new preacher found him, an unsaved man himself, and a stumbling stone to many others.

L. was too wise a preacher to publicly expose and lash an individual in the audience, especially in view of the history of the case. He felt he needed some ground to stand on to accomplish what he desired; and praying much for divine guidance, swept quickly through mere acquaintanceship into friendly and kindly relations with the man whose soul he was after.

As it happened, in a few weeks L.'s family went away on a visit for a month, and naturally the pastor received invitations from his members to eat and sleep at their different homes. The one he was burning to obtain came towards the last, and was cordially accepted. He was to take supper and breakfast and spend the night at a place he was sorely needed.

The man of God was much on his knees all the afternoon that preceded that important visit, where not only a soul but souls were at stake. Of course the transgressor and church law breaker could be tried and promptly cast out from the membership, and this would have to be done if his plan failed. But the preacher's heart sank at the thought that even this proceeding, right as it was, would mean a lost soul, and the liquor business still going on, and numbers of men falling into hell as a consequence of the continued traffic. Oh, if God would be gracious to him, and anoint his lips, and bless his very manner, and help him to order his case, that the Devil might be defeated, a crushing life burden lifted from a woman's heart, a man's feet plucked from the brink of hell and a great victory won for Heaven that would bless not only one family but scores and hundreds of others! This was the man's constant thought, and equally fervent heart cry and prayer.

It would be difficult to describe that social and pastoral visit combined. Taught and helped by God, the preacher made great advances into the esteem and affection of both husband and wife.

After supper was over, and sitting in the pleasant library the painful subject of the man's business was brought up so naturally and easily that no one could tell how it had been effected.

At once the host took the alarm and threw up his fortifications with the old time-worn excuses, and arguments of sophistry; but the guest with quiet manner, gentle voice, heart all warm with the Holy Spirit, and brain and tongue alert and touched of Heaven, levelled every breastwork, spiked every gun, got possession of the flag and quietly surrounded the silenced enemy.

With a husky voice and eyes filled with tears the preacher added:

"There is something more about the case that I have not yet referred to; and it is bound to come close to your heart, for it will affect the welfare and happiness of those who are nearest and dearest to you. Do you know, my brother, that the Bible says 'Woe to the man who putteth the bottle to his neighbors' lips'? This woe is certain to come, for all God's warnings and threats take place. His word never fails. The 'woe' spoken of in the Scripture may fall upon you, or upon your family. If it comes on you, it will crush them; and if it overtakes them, that will crush you. In either case you are doomed. Then above all remember that you are diametrically opposed in your life and business, to the work and business of Jesus Christ, the Son of God. He is trying to save men, and you are endeavoring to ruin and damn them."

*   *   *   *   *   *

The house in which the preacher was entertained was a three-story brick dwelling. The first floor was devoted to the liquor traffic, mainly a wholesale business; the second consisted of parlor, sitting room, dining room and bed chambers, while the guest was given an apartment in the third story looking out upon the street.

With heart all stirred and brain fired by the conversation and scenes in the library, the preacher after retiring found it impossible to sleep. He tossed and turned an hundred times, but unable to compose himself to slumber listened hour after hour to the striking of distant town clocks.

More than once through the night he imagined he heard strange rumbling sounds in the house, but dismissed the thought as a fancy and continued his restless exercise.

Just before day, however, he was so certain that he heard a jarring noise on the pavement, and that something unusual was taking place in or near the building, that he arose and glancing downward through the closed blinds of his window, beheld to his amazement several long rows of whisky barrels ranged on the brick walk and in the street immediately in front of the store. As he stood wondering at the sight he saw his host appear at the door with still another cask which he rolled into line with the rest. After this he disappeared and was gone several minutes, when he returned with an axe in his hand, and took his station at the head of one of the lines of barrels.

The starlight had that indistinctness peculiar to the coming of the day, but still every attitude and motion of the man was plainly discernible by the preacher.

Suddenly he saw him raise the axe and with a tremendous blow stove in the head of the first barrel, when with a great g-u-s-h, the red whisky poured over the pavement, ran into the gutter and flowed away in the direction of the river. Stepping up to the second cask, the axe again rose and fell, a second barrel head crashed in and sixty more gallons of the crimson liquid of hell which brutalizes and beggarizes the household, breaks the hearts of women, bruises the bodies of innocent children and damns the souls of men, went on its rushing way through the ditch towards the Mississippi.

The man never hesitated, but went on smashing cask after cask, until five thousand dollars, every cent of his stock in trade, had poured into the gutter, and swirled and swept on its way through the street to the river.

Day was breaking in the East when he had completed his work, and day was breaking in him at the same time. He stood leaning on his axe contemplating the scene of havoc before him, ignorant that he himself was being beheld and rejoiced over from the third window. Then there was still another window, much higher, and opening from Heaven itself, that we feel convinced was crowded with angelic and redeemed faces looking on in joy at a man who impoverished himself for the truth's sake, and became poor that he might get right and rich with God.

He stood still for a full minute as if studying his own work, and then looked up to the sky! The light was in the East, and a brighter light was in his face. Pardon and peace had come to him when he struck the last blow on the last barrel; and now for the first time in his life he could give the upward gaze to Heaven, assured that it was received, and thrilled with the consciousness that it was returned by Him who dwelt in the sky. It had cost him all that he possessed to obtain the upward look, but judging from the happiness that was then beaming in his face, he had come out gainer in the transaction beyond figures in arithmetic to compute and words in any language to describe.

May God in His mercy, grant us all the power, to cast The Upward Look.

XXVII.

The Power of a Dream

Just how and why dreams come is one of the mysteries of life. About the time we conclude that they are a projection of one's waking thoughts, comes a midnight vision of the most unique and fantastic pattern, and dealing with things that we never thought of before nor had concerning them the faintest imagination. There is also a difference of opinion as to their moral value. Some may be sent by God; while with others He unquestionably has nothing to do. In the olden days the Lord evidently made use of dreams for the comfort, direction, and deliverance of His people. In the present time with an open Bible in the hand, and the recognized leadings of the Holy Spirit in the life, we do not need these strange flitting mental pictures of the night to show us our duty, privilege or danger, as was done to men in an earlier dispensation that was far less favored than ours. Nevertheless there are times when the ordinary means of grace seem utterly to fail with certain individuals, and Heaven in its efforts to arouse and save the immortal soul, is driven to the employment of methods unusual and extraordinary. So we doubt not that there are dreams sent as directly to the slumberer on the bed, as a sermon to the sleeping conscience in the pew, or as a prophet has been directed to a sinful city, with a message of warning or woe.

In harmony with this thought, we recall the experiences related in our hearing of three preachers who are as widely removed in temperament as they are in the localities where they reside.

One of these men was greatly gifted in speech, possessed charming manners, and became a kind of pulpit and social idol with his congregation. The incense burned continually to him, intoxicated his brain, drove the grace out of his heart and finally ascended like a fog around a backslider with a clergyman's coat on his back and a shining beaver hat on his head. At the very time his gold chain was glittering most, his rattan whirling gracefully in the air, and his people were highest in their praises of him, he was without Christ and Ichabod was written on the walls of his soul.

To this man, God sent a dream of the Judgment Day. As he lay one night locked in slumber on his pillow he beheld the world on fire, the rolling flames towering above the clouds, while he heard frantic stricken multitudes crying out, "The Judgment Day has come! The Judgment Day has come!"

At this moment in his sleep he seemed to lift up his eyes and see the Son of God descending through the Heavens. In his agony he ran, so that the Saviour's face might be turned upon him, and to his amazement the Lord averted His countenance. Rushing around in that direction to his unspeakable consternation Christ turned His face from him the second time; and this was repeated again with such an unmistakable expression of displeasure, that the preacher woke up with his face wet with tears, sobbing, "He won't look at me! He won't look at me!"

That vision brought the gifted man down in deepest humiliation, penitence and prayer before God. He was heard in Heaven in that he feared, and the restored servant of Christ has been blazing in a skyward way ever since.

A second ministerial friend of the writer admitted publicly that in the active life of a pastor, preaching, visiting and flying around generally, he lost God. He continued to go on his rounds, baptized the children, married the people, delivered his sermons, made his announcements and took up the conference collections; but for all that he was a backslider. A dead man was in the pulpit talking to dead men on the pews. A corpse was driving a loaded hearse to the cemetery.

At this juncture came the dream. The vision showed him to be in Hell. He was rolling in agony amid billows of torturing fire. With fearful struggles he struck out for a shore which he saw in the distance. As he came nearer he beheld his mother standing on the bank gazing with anguish upon him as though she would help her gasping, laboring son out of his torment. Just as he reached the strand, and stretched forth his hand to pull himself upon the beach, the Devil suddenly appeared, coming over the bank, with a look of infernal joy and malicious triumph. He whirled a whip of fire in his hand, the lash of which seemed to be a mile long, curling and flickering like a streak of lightning. He brought it down upon the unhappy man with a sharp detonating crack, and the keen quivering thong seemed to penetrate body and soul alike with an agony beyond any words to describe. With an awful groan he fell back in the billows of flame, hearing the Devil's shout of victory, and the broken hearted wail of his mother, as she cried "My poor boy!" "My poor boy!"

This dreadful experience was gone through with three times; when the mental distress, and the actual suffering of body became so great through the vivid, life-like dream, that the preacher burst through the gates of slumber with a piercing cry to God for help and mercy, and fell with sobs and tears, face downward, upon the floor.

Today he is one of the holiest men known to the writer.

The third instance is that of a preacher who after years of diligent, faithful service in the Christian life, began gradually to grow weary of its constant cross bearing and self-denial. The joy once realized in enduring the hardness of a good soldier of Jesus Christ subsided. The flesh cried out for a letting up, or for more indulgence; while strange inner voices called attention to the drudgery of the work, the prevalence of the commonplace, the uninteresting class of people with whom he labored, and the many instances of fruitless, resultless toil among them as far as human eye could perceive, and human wisdom judge. With all this came fierce temptations to downright fleshliness; when suddenly one night he dreamed a dream.

He seemed to be in the outskirts of a large field in what is called a "deadening." Although asleep he thought in his slumber that he had just awakened and found himself lying on the ground and completely surrounded by what seemed to be logs. Some were, and some were not; for as he gazed upon the objects he saw that a number had an almost imperceptible motion like that of a worm. What he had taken for fallen trees were huge creatures eight to ten feet long, shaped somewhat like snails, with broad bands of yellow and dusky red around their bodies. Some were lying on tree trunks not much larger than themselves, and others were stretched on the ground. Most of them were asleep, and but for a slight palpitation of the side would have looked to be dead. A few seemed to be making efforts to arouse themselves as shown in quivering eyelid and lazy stretching of muscle. One had opened his great flabby mouth in a yawn which disclosed a crimson cavity down which a man could easily have disappeared. Others were awake and had a slow vermicular motion toward the preacher that was simply horrifying in its deliberateness. In addition, the eyes of all the awakened ones were resting on the unhappy man who, paralyzed with fear, lay helpless in their midst. The moral horror and spiritual loathing felt in the vision, surpassed the physical terror realized in the case of nightmare. The spectacle of a creeping, crawling fleshliness, with no mind in its dull eyes, no heart or soul in its gross form, but a mere shape of the lowest plane of physical life, moving toward him with an enswathement and accompaniment of fat and oiliness, of laziness, sleepiness and stupidity, so terrified the slumbering minister, that he cried out in agony. He awoke with a staring eyed, open mouthed horror, to find his face bathed in a cold clammy sweat, and his body trembling as with an ague.

He felt as he collected his faculties and tried to think, that God had caused him to look on symbolized materialism; on the carnal mind incarnated. He was convinced that he had been shown in a terrible picture the trend and end of the soul which turns from God, truth, and spiritual things to walk in gross and fleshly lines. That a spirit finally animalized becomes as unlike a man, as a fallen devil fails to resemble one of God's holy angels.

The shock that night was terrific, but something of the kind was needed.

Suffice it to say that the dream accomplished that whereunto it was sent; a delusion was swept away; a faltering soul was steadied; and the adversary exposed, foiled, discomfited and defeated once more by the Son of God.

So in the three instances related God accomplished a wonderful work through a vision of the night. Recovery and salvation was the result in each case.

Of course it is easy to criticize these incidents and say they are too realistic, that they are nerve shocking, and also offensive to the best taste. Complaint also might be made that the imagery used is too gross for the proper description of spiritual states, and utterly inadequate to depict conditions in another world that is so different from anything we know in life.

In reply we ask what figures and images have we used that are not also found in the Bible. There we read of the Lake of Fire, of unquenchable flames, of undying worms, of a being who has become a dragon, of a worldliness that is like a red beast, of weeping, wailing and gnashing of teeth, of Christ coming in the clouds, of the world being on fire, of a bottomless pit, and all enthroned in Hell, a tormenting Devil.

As for dreams, far more wonderful ones than the three we have related are recorded in the Word of God. So all these objections viewed in the light of Scripture alone, are found to go down.

Then let it be remembered that this life sketch was not written to defend dreams nor even to explain them. The chapter is simply to tell of three remarkable occurrences; how a preacher was getting off the narrow way upon the broad way that leads to death; and how two others were off entirely and heading rapidly for ruin; when God sent the visions as described and saved the three men. The only point we make is that the dreams came, and the men were saved.

XXVIII.

A Night Visitor

The preacher had slipped away by a side door of the Tabernacle from the throng that was thanking him for his sermons, and bidding him farewell. He had regained his room, and, flushed and gratified with the pleasant things that had been said to him that night, he leaned his head upon his hand, and the mind took a sweet review of faces as well as speeches of the closing hour.

Looking at his watch he saw that he had time to dash off a letter to a certain religious paper, and deposit it in a letter-box before the last round of the mail collector. So, drawing up a small table, and with hat tilted backward on his head, he wrote the following lines with flying pen:

"Mr. Editor:

"At the meeting previous to this last one, just closed tonight, I had a wonderful victory. It was a hard place, but I poured in Sinai shot and shell after the hottest manner and things went all to pieces. On the fifth day the opposition melted like mists before the morning sun, and the whole community was stirred from center to circumference and went down before the Great Flood of Salvation.

"From that place I came to this city of three hundred thousand inhabitants. Immediately upon my arrival I saw that the holiness professed here was of the sloppiest character; so I went for everything in sight, and preached the straight truth. As a result, on the fifth day the people got their eyes opened for the first time, and began to sweep into genuine holiness. Other great teachers and preachers had been here, but nothing has ever been seen like my meeting.

"The building in which the meetings were held was crowded to suffocation; thousands of people were in our street services and could not get into the hall where we held forth. The scenes around the altar defied description. Gales of Glory, Tornadoes of Power, Johnstown Floods, Waterspouts and a Noah's Deluge of Salvation swept the audience, while perfect Cyclones of Conviction fell on the people at every service. Lawyers, doctors, merchants, editors, professors and members of the Legislature and of Congress swept with shouts and cries into the Fountain. The whole city was stirred! The oldest inhabitants say they never witnessed such a revival.

"Men raged, and the opposition was intense. But everything went down before us. The Devil was sent howling back to Hell. Eternity alone can reveal the good that was done in this meeting.

"Hundreds were at the altar. Great numbers swept into the Fountain, and it is safe to say that hundreds, if not thousands, were turned from the doors unable to get in. Hundreds followed me to the train, and begged me to come again. If I can, I will.

"I leave early in the morning for a city that has been trying to get me for a year, but so numerous are my calls that I could not go until now. Will write you from that point. Pray for me.

"Your humble brother,
"A. BLOHART."

The letter was folded and addressed, and Brother Blohart, stepping quickly out, dropped it in a letterbox in front of the hotel, letting the iron lid strike twice to be sure that the valuable document was inside and safe.

Returning to his room, after leaving orders at the office to be called at 6 o'clock for the early train, the preacher packed his valise, disrobed himself, and, forgetting to pray, flung himself upon the bed and sought sleep.

But somehow the desired slumber would not come. Thought was on fire; the brain cells were surcharged with blood; faces, voices, speeches, handclasps, flatteries of all kinds were fairly rioting together in his mind. For two hours he had tossed, and pleasant retrospection was mightier than somnolency. His mental pictures were so vivid that he was kept awake looking at them. He wanted to go to sleep and didn't want to go. And so he tossed on, sometimes smiling in the dark as words of praise came back to him, and sometimes sighing as an uneasy, troubled feeling touched his spirit.

Twelve o'clock had long ago sounded, and the last wheel of belated carriage and wagon had ceased to echo from the deserted street. Now and then only, the distant stroke of the policeman's club, as it descended with ringing sound upon the pavement, fell upon his ear. The city was asleep. The people who had flattered him were locked in slumber and had long ago forgotten him, and yet here he was, brooding upon their fulsome utterances.

The hour of one struck from a remote town clock. How solemnly it sounded! A change already seemed to have taken place in the Past. The scenes of the evening had been gone over so frequently in his mind that they were beginning to pall upon him. He felt something akin to disgust creeping in his heart. Then that solitary note of the bell sounded so strangely like a knell. His room seemed to hold the echo for a full minute, and then became silent and oppressive, like a tomb. The sensation was like to the feeling which comes over one when a funeral procession has swept past and left the street deserted.

Suddenly the preacher became conscious that there was another Presence in the room. With a thrill of fear he glanced up and saw a shrouded Form standing at the foot of his bed and obviously looking at him. Just then an electric light on the street gave one of its periodic glares, and the apartment was for a moment illuminated, and the preacher saw the grave, white face of the Form and felt its burning eyes fixed upon him.

"Do you know me?" asked the Figure.

"Yes," replied the man of God, in a faint voice.

"I have come to have a talk with you."

The preacher was silent, and his heart sank within him.

"I have been waiting quite a while until you could recover from your excitement, become quiet and listen to me. God has sent me, and I have a message that may not be as pleasant as some things said to you by thoughtless people tonight; but it will be more profitable."

The preacher gave a heavy sigh and said, "Say on."

"You mailed a letter tonight to a Holiness paper; and you wrote it as a Holiness man?"

"Yes."

"What made you tell those untruths in it?"

(Profound silence in the room and on the bed.)

"You said in that letter that you came from a town where the opposition melted like mists before the morning sun, and the place was shaken from center to circumference. Now answer me as God's representative, what were the results of your whole meeting?"

No reply.

"Answer me, as you will have to do at the Day of Judgment?"

"Two young people were reclaimed," replied the evangelist, in an almost inaudible whisper.

"And yet you wrote as though a mighty revival had visited the town!"

No word from the bed.

The White Figure looked steadily at the prostrate man for quite a while and resumed:

"You wrote tonight that on coming to this city, of three hundred thousand inhabitants, you discovered on the very first day that the Holiness professed here was of the sloppiest character. How was it possible for you to know such a thing as that on the first day, unless you were God Himself?"

No answer.

"You wrote that the hall was crowded to suffocation. How many people could it accommodate?"

Continued silence.

"Answer me; you know I have the power to make you admit the truth, and truth is what I want tonight. How many people could be accommodated in the hall?"

"Two hundred."

"And yet you conveyed in your letter the idea that a great audience was listening to you."

"I feel that I did wrong," said the preacher.

"Then you wrote that thousands were in the street. Did you count them?"

"No."

"Do you know that it is the rarest thing for a religious street meeting to number over two hundred persons?"

More silence.

"You stated most confidently that the whole city was stirred by your meeting. That is, that a great metropolis was moved mightily by your meeting, when not one person in two hundred or five hundred knew you were there."

"I feel now that I exaggerated and deplore my hasty utterances."

The Figure looked steadily at the man before him for a while, and said:

"God will have to forgive you for the falsehood which you call an exaggeration. My business is to show you where your letter was false. God has sent me to speak with you about it."

Some heavy sighs came from the bed.

"Who was that oldest inhabitant that said your meeting was the greatest ever held in that city?"

"Several of the brethren told me they thought so."

"Were they the oldest inhabitants?"

"No."

"So you lied again?"

An awful groan from the bed.

"Did you witness the Johnstown flood?"

"No."

"Were you ever in a real cyclone?"

"No."

"Of course you have some idea of the awful and widespread power of the things you mentioned in your letter as Gales, Tornadoes and Deluges?"

"I have read about them."

"You wrote that you had just such things in spiritual lines in your meeting; that God worked on such scales and grades of omnipotence."

A profound silence.

"In the Johnstown flood," continued the Figure, "thousands were killed, millions of property swept away, and the civilized world was moved at the occurrence. At the Deluge the entire Human Race was destroyed with the exception of a single family. And yet you said you had a Johnstown Flood and a Noah's Deluge in your meeting."

A heavy sigh from the bed.

"How many people were really saved and sanctified in this last meeting? Answer me as you will have to answer God at the last Day."

The preacher turned restlessly.

"I am waiting," said the Form; "tell me the number that you think in your heart were really saved?"

"Between thirty and forty."

"And yet you wrote that hundreds were at the altar, and that great numbers swept into the Fountain of Cleansing."

More tossing on the bed.

"You spoke of the Devil being sent howling back to Hell; did you hear him howl?"

Profound silence.

"Did you ever hear him howl?"

No word of reply.

"You wrote about Hell raging against you, and the human opposition being so intense. Who opposed you?"

No answer.

"Did the city authorities stop your meeting?"

"No."

"Did the church forbid you?"

"No."

"Did the press say anything against you?"

"The papers ignored us."

"Did anyone in the audience cry out against you, and mobs break up your services?"

"No."

"Well, where was the 'intense opposition' you wrote about?"

"Several people were overheard talking on the street, saying they did not believe in sanctification and others laughed at my mannerisms, as they called my style of preaching."

"But your mannerisms are not Holiness."

"No, but another man said that such loud, noisy meetings ought to be stopped."

"Is that all?"

"Y—e—s."

"Do you call that intense opposition?"

No reply.

"Do you know what they did to Paul?"

"They scourged and stoned him."

"Do you remember what the people did to Wesley?"

"They frequently stoned and mobbed him."

"What did the people do to Christ?"

"They killed Him."

"What is there to compare between their sufferings and yours?"

"Nothing—absolutely nothing," groaned the man on the bed.

"One striking difference was that hundreds, you say, went to the depot to see you off, while with the apostle and the Saviour, hundreds went with them outside the city walls to stone or crucify them."

There was a silence of minutes, and then the Figure resumed:

"With the light of Heaven and Truth shining upon you, what are you tonight?"

"A hypocrite and a liar!" cried out the preacher, and burst into tears.

The instant the Figure heard the sound of weeping, his whole manner changed and became full of tenderness. Going softly to the door he admitted another white Form, and coming back to the bedside with the new visitor, stooped down over the penitent man of God, whose face was covered with his hands, and whispered:

"Do you know me?"

"Yes."

"Who am I?"

"Conscience."

"Yes, I am Conscience, your true friend. I have not desired to pain you needlessly; but to warn you."

"You have nearly broken my heart," sighed the man of God.

"Do you suppose," returned the Figure, "that I have thus dealt with you simply to make you suffer?"

"Oh, no," replied the preacher, "you could not do that. I know it was all for my correction and good, and that you have done right."

"Do you remember that the Bible speaks of a lying spirit getting into a prophet?"

"Yes."

"Do you want to be thus possessed?"

"God forbid."

"Do you remember who it was that said 'Let your conversation be yea, yea, nay, nay, and whatsoever is more than these cometh of evil'?"

"Yes, I know Him and love Him."

"Would you not prefer to please Him?"

The tears filled the eyes of the preacher and flowed rapidly down his cheeks, as he said humbly and fervently:

"I want to be like Him in all things."

Conscience smiled approvingly and lovingly upon the penitent, and said:

"God has sent someone else to see you, who bears a blessed message to your soul from Him."

"Who is it?" he asked, looking up.

And the second white Form bent over him and pressed a kiss upon the tear-stained cheek, and replied:

"My name is Mercy."

And the man's face fairly glowed in the shadows of the room, while happy smiles and equally happy tears strove for mastery on the illumined countenance.

And so, by and by, he fell asleep murmuring:

"Blessed Saviour! from this hour I will act, speak, write and do all things like Thee."

Conscience and Mercy stood a while looking at the tired, slumbering servant of God, smiled upon him and at each other, shook hands, and went to their own places. Meanwhile the preacher had sunk into a profound, refreshing sleep, such as God has promised His beloved. Every care was forgotten, the heart was at rest, and the reflection of a glad smile made his face look as if the light of childhood's innocent, happy, sunny hours had fallen upon him once more.